UNDP/UNFPA/WHO/World Bank
Special Programme of Research, Development
and Research Training in Human Reproduction
(HRP)

Biennial Report
1994–1995

UNDP/UNFPA/WHO/World Bank
Special Programme of Research, Development
and Research Training in Human Reproduction
(HRP)

Biennial Report
1994–1995

World Health Organization
Geneva
1996

In order to ensure prompt distribution, this Report is being issued without the usual detailed editorial revision by the WHO Office of Publications.

WHO Library Cataloguing in Publication Data

UNDP / UNFPA / WHO / World Bank Special Programme of Research, Development and Research Training in Human Reproduction.
Biennial Report : 1994–1995.

I.Reproduction 2.Research 3.Contraception 4.Fertility 5.Family planning

ISBN 92 4 156183 1   (NLM Classification: WP 630)

The World Health Organization welcomes requests for permission to reproduce or translate its publications, in part or in full. Applications and enquiries should be addressed to the Office of Publications, World Health Organization, Geneva, Switzerland, which will be glad to provide the latest information on any changes made to the text, plans for new editions, and reprints and translations already available.

The designations employed and the presentations of the material in this publication do not imply the expression of any opinion whatsoever on the part of the Secretariat of the World Health Organization concerning the legal status of any country, territory, city or area or of its authorities, or concerning the delimitation of its frontiers or boundaries.

The mention of specific companies or of certain manufacturers' products does not imply that they are endorsed or recommended by the World Health Organization in preference to others of a similar nature that are not mentioned. Errors and omissions excepted, the names of proprietary products are distinguished by initial capital letters.

Contents

Preface

During the 1994–1995 biennium, two major United Nations conferences helped to keep reproductive health firmly on the international agenda. First, in September 1994, the International Conference on Population and Development (ICPD), held in Cairo, Egypt, anchored the issue of population and development resolutely in health. Second, in September 1995 in Beijing, China, the Fourth World Conference on Women focused on women's health and well-being, emphasizing especially women's reproductive health needs and rights.

The new emphasis placed on reproductive health by the two meetings has created new opportunities and challenges for the Special Programme of Research, Development and Research Training in Human Reproduction (HRP). For example, the ICPD Programme of Action has called for an increased commitment to, and support for, reproductive health research, including: generation of reliable information on issues of safety and effectiveness of fertility regulating methods; an intensified effort in biomedical and social science research that will enable men to take a greater responsibility for reproductive health; and research to develop contraceptive methods which can be controlled by users and which can provide protection against sexually transmitted diseases including HIV/AIDS.

Thus, during the biennium, along with ongoing activities, HRP took decisive steps to reposition its research mission and goals in line with the calls made by ICPD and the World Conference on Women. HRP staff developed, for consideration by the Programme's Policy and Coordination Committee (PCC), a new vision for HRP as well as new mission goals. As per the new vision statement, HRP sees its role as a leader in international reproductive health research with a dynamic research strategy sensitive to people's changing needs. The mission goals, which reflect the ICPD consensus, require HRP to commit itself to improving global reproductive health by:

- increasing informed choices in reproductive health for women;
- increasing male responsibility in reproductive health;
- responding to the needs of developing countries in research and capacity strengthening for research in reproductive health;
- coordinating and expanding the global research effort.

In 1995 PCC endorsed HRP's vision and mission goals and revised the Programme's mandate. The new mandate acknowledges that HRP is the main instrument within the United Nations system for "promoting, conducting, evaluating and coordinating interdisciplinary research on reproductive health, for collaborating with countries in enhancing national capacities to conduct such research, for promoting the use of research results in policy-making and planning for reproductive health care at national and international levels, and for the setting of standards and guidelines, including ethical guidelines, in the field of reproductive health research".

Also during the biennium, the cause of reproductive health received yet another boost from the creation within WHO of the new programme area of Family and Reproductive Health (FRH). With a view to strengthening links between reproductive health research and application of research findings, HRP was brought under the FRH umbrella. Now HRP will be able to work even more closely with the Division of Reproductive Health Technical Support (formerly the Division of Family Health)—the Division entrusted to convert research findings into pragmatic advice and action. Functioning within the new structure and equipped with a new vision, mission goals, and mandate, HRP is ready to take on the challenges, and take advantage of the opportunities, that have emerged from the global focus on reproductive health.

The vision and mission statements, the new mandate, HRP's comparative advantages and how the Programme is restructuring itself to take advantage of the opportunities and to face the challenges can all be found in this report in the chapter entitled "Adapting to meet the challenges of the future".

One new strategy adopted by HRP to reach its goals has been to replace the more rigid discipline-based research with a more target-oriented approach. As a result, HRP staff have now started to work as members of interdisciplinary teams. To some extent this new interdisciplinary approach is reflected in the presentation of this biennial report. Rather than the usual chapters such as "epidemiological research" and "social science research", in this report the readers will find chapter titles that better describe what HRP really does and seeks to achieve: Surveying reproductive health, Assessing and improving reproductive health services, Understanding people's reproductive health needs and perspectives, Expanding family planning options, Evaluating safety and efficacy of family planning methods, Developing new methods of fertility regulation, and Building reproductive health research capacity in developing countries. We hope this approach will enable readers, especially policy-makers and non-scientists, to have a better understanding of HRP's work. Furthermore, in order to present to the reader the highlights of the biennium and their implications at a glance, each chapter opens with a short, easy-to-read section entitled "Highlights".

We hope the readers will find this presentation helpful.

Giuseppe Benagiano
Director

Paul F.A. Van Look
Associate Director

Surveying reproductive health

Highlights

• Studies on the prevalence of lower genital tract infection with *Chlamydia trachomatis* are being conducted in selected populations in Chile, China, Indonesia, Malaysia, and Viet Nam. Studies in other countries are also planned.

HRP is committed to improving reproductive health, especially in developing countries. An aspect of reproductive health that has remained largely neglected is the large number of reproductive tract infections, especially in women, which if left untreated can lead to serious health problems. The main objectives of HRP in this area are:

Information on the epidemiology of sexually transmitted diseases (STDs) in developing countries is practically nonexistent. Studies on the prevalence of active chlamydial and gonococcal lower genital tract infections in selected populations—both high-risk and low-risk—can provide valuable information for devising prevention strategies.

• to determine the prevalence of genital tract infections in selected populations;

• to conduct epidemiological studies on lower genital tract infection; and

• to determine the prevalence of chlamydial infection in adolescent males.

• In a study of 400 women in Hanoi, Viet Nam, the prevalence of chlamydial infection was 3.7% in women with symptoms of infection and 3.4% in women who did not have any symptoms; candidiasis was common in both groups (22.2% and 23.6%, respectively) and *Trichomonas* vaginitis less so (5.3% and 0.6%, respectively).

This study shows a high prevalence of candidiasis in both women with no symptoms as well as those who have symptoms.

• Several studies are under way on the prevalence of chlamydial infection in adolescent men. In one study in Chile, the prevalence of chlamydial urethritis was 3.2% in sexually active male adolescents; no gonococcal infections were detected.

Sexually active male adolescents are a major source of chlamydial genital tract infection in young women. This study emphasizes the need to include also young people as a target group for information on STD prevention.

Prevalence of sexually transmitted disease

Each year some 333 million people worldwide become infected with a curable sexually transmitted disease (STD). STDs are preventable and—except for STDs caused by viruses such as human immunodeficiency virus (HIV) or the human papilloma virus (HPV)—are curable. But in many cases these diseases remain undetected and untreated, causing serious health problems, including infertility.

Two common organisms responsible for STDs are *Chlamydia trachomatis* and *Neisseria gonorrhoeae*. They can cause salpingitis (inflammation of the Fallopian tubes) and pelvic infection, resulting in blockage of the Fallopian tubes, pelvic adhesions, infertility and chronic pelvic pain. *Chlamydia* causes more severe subclinical inflammation and subsequent damage to the Fallopian tubes than other bacteria.

There are few studies in developing countries on the prevalence of chlamydial infection. These studies suggest that the relative contributions of chlamydial and gonococcal infection to diseases of the Fallopian tubes are possibly different from developed countries with a higher proportion of past gonococcal disease. There is a need to collect further data on the prevalence of chlamydial lower genital tract infection in women with particular emphasis on developing countries in Asia and Latin America. HRP is conducting such studies in selected populations and through gynaecological health surveys.

Chlamydial lower genital tract infection in selected populations

Information on the epidemiology of STDs in developing countries is very limited. In spite of this, prevalence studies on active chlamydial and gonococcal lower genital tract infections in selected populations—both high-risk and low-risk—can point towards epidemiological patterns.

Chile

In Santiago, 236 out of a total of 250 male partners of infertile couples have been investigated for asymptomatic chlamydial urethritis, using urine samples for antigen detection. This group forms part of a project on the role of chlamydial infection and sperm function. Final results are expected by mid-1996.

China

Although STDs are not as common in China as in other Asian countries, it is believed that they are on the rise. A survey in an STD clinic in Beijing in 1989 showed 23% of men with non-gonococcal urethritis to have chlamydial infection and 63% of women attending the clinic to have chlamydial cervicitis. In late 1994, an HRP study in Beijing started on men and women attending an STD clinic, women with symptoms of pelvic inflammatory disease and pregnant women. The study is designed to detect *Neisseria gonorrhoeae* and *Chlamydia trachomatis*. In the sample of 200 pregnant women, the prevalence of chlamydial infection was 2% and there were no cases of gonorrhoea. In a group of 250 male and female patients attending an STD clinic, 14.7% were positive for *Chlamydia*

trachomatis and 26.5% positive for *Neisseria gonorrhoeae*. This study is continuing.

HRP is also undertaking a project in Shanghai in which 456 women having an induced abortion matched with 456 women attending a family planning clinic will be examined for infection with *Neisseria gonorrhoeae* and *Chlamydia trachomatis*. This study will be completed in 1996.

A multicentre study is planned to start in 1996 in China in which 1622 subjects will be recruited in each of three cities (Kunming, Shanghai and Shenzhen) making a total of 4866 subjects. The main purpose of the study is to investigate the prevalence of gonorrhoea and *Chlamydia* infection in specific population groups in more developed cities in China and risk factors of STD transmission. The population groups to be investigated are patients attending STD clinics, women attending family planning clinics, commercial sex workers and their clients.

Indonesia

In Indonesia, centres in Surabaya and Ujung Pandang will investigate the prevalence of *Neisseria gonorrhoeae* and *Chlamydia trachomatis* in both partners of infertile couples, patients with ectopic pregnancy, pregnant women, men and women attending an STD clinic and a group of 300 female commercial sex workers. It is expected that these studies will be under way by early 1996.

Malaysia

In Kuala Lumpur 184 subjects (31 women with symptoms of genital tract infection, 59 women

without symptoms of infection and 94 men with symptoms) have been recruited to a comparative study of the detection of chlamydial genital tract infection. Final results are expected by mid-1996.

Viet Nam

In Hanoi a project funded by the United Nations Population Fund (UNFPA) with technical support from HRP was completed during the biennium. Women complaining of vaginal discharge and an appropriate control group of women who did not have any symptoms were screened for gonococcal and chlamydial infection as well as bacterial vaginal infection. A total of 400 women were recruited to the study. No gonococcal infections were found and the prevalence of chlamydial infection was 3.7% in the women with symptoms and 3.4% in the women who did not show any symptoms. Candidiasis was common in both groups (22.2% and 23.6%, respectively) and *Trichomonas* vaginitis less so (5.3% and 0.6%, respectively). There was a poor correlation between the patients' complaints of vaginal discharge and its characteristics on the one hand, and the presence of microorganisms, on the other.

Epidemiology of reproductive health

Over the years little attention has been given to the sexual and reproductive health of women. In poor communities around the world, reproductive tract infections (RTIs) are thought to be common and the consequences for the health and social well-being of women and their children are frequent and potentially serious. Among pregnant women in developing countries, gonorrhoea rates are 10–15 times higher, *Chlamydia* rates two-three times higher, and syphilis rates 10–100 times higher, than among pregnant women in developed countries.

During the biennium, HRP supported three studies on the reproductive health of specific communities.

Thailand

In northern Thailand, a study in the rural areas of Chiang Mai province is assessing the prevalence of gynaecological diseases and STDs in women aged between 15 and 55 years. In addition, the association of the gynaecological diseases with women's demographic characteristics, accessibility to medical services and knowledge and attitudes of the women towards STD are being investigated. Results from this study are expected by mid-1996.

Another study is also under way in north-eastern Thailand in which 599 subjects have been recruited. Preliminary results show relatively low prevalence rates of candidiasis (11%), trichomoniasis (5%) and syphilis (3%). No cases of gonorrhoea were found. Data on the prevalence of *Chlamydia*, human papilloma and herpes simplex viruses will be available in early 1996.

Papua New Guinea

In Papua New Guinea, in collaboration with the National Medical Research Council, a community-based study of 240 women and 240 in men the country's Highlands started in late 1994. The

objectives are to determine the prevalence and etiology of STDs among women, the prevalence of *Chlamydia trachomatis* infection in men, the risk factors for STDs, and the correlation between symptoms and the final diagnoses. A total of 225 women and 177 men have been recruited as well as 264 women and 87 men who presented themselves for examination without being formally selected for the study. There was a high prevalence of STDs in both groups of women (57.4%). In the men there was an overall prevalence of chlamydial urethritis of 24.4%.

Prevalence of chlamydial infection in adolescent men

With the lowering of the mean age at first sexual intercourse, particularly in male adolescents, in many societies, increasing numbers of young men are contracting chlamydial urethritis, which may not produce any symptoms in up to 80% of cases, and this group is probably a major source of chlamydial genital tract infection in the adolescent or young woman.

During the biennium, four studies on the prevalence of chlamydial urethritis in sexually experienced adolescent men were under way and three more are planned for 1996. A total of 350 adolescent men have been recruited from three vocational schools in Bangkok. Results are expected in early 1996.

Similar studies in northern Thailand have recruited 500 adolescent men and in southern Thailand 360.

In Santiago, Chile, a study

involving 154 symptomless adolescent men was completed in 1995, in which urine specimens were tested for *Chlamydia* and *Neisseria gonorrhoeae*. The average age of the men was 18 years and 39% were sexually active. The prevalence of chlamydial urethritis was 3.2% in the sexually active group and there were no gonococcal infections detected.

In Rosario, Argentina, a study of 262 adolescent men with symptoms and 173 without symptoms will start in early 1996. Urine samples will be tested for Chlamydia.

Also, a total of 912 adolescents in Mexico City and in San Luis Potosí will have urine samples tested for chlamydial antigen in a project that will start in early 1996. Up to 500 adolescent men will enter a study in Surabaya, Indonesia, in 1996 and urine samples will be tested for *Chlamydia trachomatis*.

Assessing and improving reproductive health services

Highlights

• Stage I activities—which, *inter alia*, involve an assessment of the way family planning services are being provided in a country—were conducted in Bolivia, Brazil, South Africa, Viet Nam, and Zambia.

In **Bolivia** an important recommendation was to increase access to, and improve the provision of, family planning through the introduction of an injectable contraceptive into the public sector.

In **Brazil** no new methods were recommended for immediate introduction, but it was suggested that existing methods be made more accessible with improved quality of care.

In **South Africa** most women have access to few family planning options other than injectable contraceptives. Recommendations called for provision of better services and greater use of non-hormonal contraceptive alternatives, particularly barrier methods.

In **Viet Nam** the assessment team recommended that urgent attention should be paid to issues of better counselling and greater technical expertise with existing methods and to the introduction of DMPA (depot-medroxyprogesterone acetate).

In **Zambia**, the assessment team's findings led to decisions to introduce DMPA and emergency contraception more widely.

With a view to expanding contraceptive choice in developing countries, HRP, together with other relevant WHO programmes, encourages and facilitates the comprehensive assessment of family planning needs. Activities in this area cover:

• implementation of HRP's three-stage strategy for the introduction of new and underutilized methods of fertility regulation, based upon users' needs and capabilities of health care services;

• coordination of activities with other agencies to mobilize additional resources at the country level;

• development of standards and norms on the quality of products for fertility regulation and for the introduction of methods into national programmes, including ethical considerations.

• Stage II activities involve the development of the most appropriate means by which new and/or existing but underutilized methods may be best introduced or reintroduced to improve quality of care. In 1995, a project in the Sao Paulo state in Brazil focused on operational and management changes to broaden contraceptive choice and improve the quality of reproductive health services. In Viet Nam, a study is being undertaken on DMPA introduction within the context of improved quality of care in the provision of all family planning methods.

Because baseline data in **Brazil** demonstrated that family planning either did not get any attention or had the lowest priority with health providers, a municipality-based study is addressing the organizational and management changes required for appropriate provision of services. A key aspect of this project is the dissemination of project information, with constant contact being maintained with officials and key community members.

In **Viet Nam**, the introduction of DMPA is addressing the quality provision of all available methods and includes training of providers (provincial and district level doctors, midwives, community health centre personnel, community-level family planning motivators, etc.) as well as development of information, education, and communication (IEC) materials for potential users.

Stage I activities
Bolivia

In Bolivia, as in other country assessments, a participatory process ensured that the assessment team's work was grounded in the local context. The team's recommendations included the need to: review the various injectable contraceptive products available in the private sector; undertake research for introducing an injectable contraceptive into the public sector; develop appropriate policies, programmes, and research for the development of community-based approaches to family planning and safe motherhood (including adolescent services); and legitimize family planning within a reproductive health approach to primary health care.

It is planned to hold a workshop involving all relevant stakeholders, which will discuss the findings and implications of the assessment as well as plans for future activities.

Brazil

In Brazil, the assessment team found limited availability of family planning services in the public sector. The Ministry of Health approved the provision of oral contraceptives, IUDs, condoms, spermicides, diaphragms, and natural methods, but few were available regularly in the public sector. The assessment team did not recommend additional methods. The team recommended that efforts be made to strengthen the provision of underutilized methods like the IUD, barrier methods, and the lactational amenorrhoea method.

South Africa

In South Africa, the assessment was done with the cooperation of a national Reproductive Health Task Force, which was created to provide inputs into the development of a national reproductive health policy in consultation with all relevant stakeholders.

South Africa had a contraceptive prevalence of greater than

The goal of HRP's work on the Introduction and Transfer of Technologies for Fertility Regulation is to undertake research to help governments in broadening options for fertility regulation, taking into account the needs of individuals and couples and the capabilities of health care services. Three stages are involved in the approach.

Stage I involves an assessment of the existing status of family planning in a country, the mix of contraceptive methods being provided, the extent of coverage and service infrastructure, as well as obtaining information on users' needs.

Stage II research activities involve the development of the most appropriate means by which new and/or underutilized methods may be best introduced or reintroduced in the context of improved quality of care. This stage involves an examination of the delivery system's ability to provide services, and users' perspectives on the service system and on the specific contraceptive technology. It addresses policy, organizational and management capabilities, as well as quality of care, suggesting changes necessary to introduce a chosen method.

Stage III applies research findings from Stage II to policy development and planning. Decisions are made as to whether or not it is appropriate to expand use of particular methods on a larger scale. If expansion is recommended, a strategic plan for providing the method throughout the family planning programme is developed. This includes preparing training plans, establishing the necessary infrastructure, providing information, education, and communication (IEC) materials, upgrading logistics systems, and organizing supply sources and possible local production.

50%. However, few women of African origin have adequate access to or a choice in contraceptive methods, particularly in the rural areas. Nearly 70% of contraceptives used were injectables. These were the providers' and users' methods of choice in underserved areas. Injectables represented 90% or more of contraceptives prescribed by mobile clinic staff. Providers felt that there was a chance that women would forget to take their oral contraceptives pills regularly and that the use of injectable contraceptives could be hidden from the male partner. A commonly held belief was that the injectable norethisterone enantate was more appropriate for teenagers and young women than the other injectable, DMPA.

Oral contraceptives were the only other method readily available through clinics. Their use, however, was discouraged and many providers misprescribed them. Neither providers nor women were aware of the possibility of using high-dose oral contraceptives, such as Ovral, for emergency contraception.

IUDs were not available except at urban centres or referral clinics in rural areas. Where they were provided, consideration was rarely given to a woman's sexually transmitted disease (STD) status.

Sterilization was not readily available. Long waiting lists existed for female sterilization in the public sector. Providers were often biased against sterilization owing to inadequate facilities, an insufficient number of trained doctors, poor operating technique leading to sterilization failure, the requirement of husband's consent in many areas (although this is not legally required), and misperception about the method's overall effectiveness. Male sterilization was virtually unheard of and, where it was known, it was rarely accepted.

Regarding barrier methods, there was little condom promotion. Condoms tended to be available only through the national AIDS programme. The diaphragm was unavailable through the public sector. Research was called for regarding female condom acceptability.

The implantable contraceptive, Norplant, was registered in South Africa and was available through the private sector. However, the necessary provider training requirements, particularly for removal and follow-up, meant that it probably would be inappropriate to provide the method beyond a certain number of urban clinics.

Overall, women did not have real access to informed contraceptive choice.

STDs were considered to be at epidemic levels. Facilities and personnel for STD prevention, diagnosis, and treatment were inadequate. In addition, reproductive tract cancer (in particular, cervical cancer) was a major problem. Infertility was not recognized as a major reproductive health problem, despite its socially disruptive nature. The number of illegal and unsafe abortions was significant. At the community level, there was considerable ignorance about the conditions under which an abortion could be done legally.

The assessment team concluded that it would be essential for South Africa to develop a series of district-based projects in several provinces. These projects should aim to identify the service delivery, administrative and operational changes that would help expand contraceptive choice through planned introduction of appropriate methods.

Viet Nam

In Viet Nam, contraceptive prevalence was close to 50%. Nearly two-thirds of contraceptive use was accounted for by IUDs. Although there was vast experience with both CuT380A and Multiload 375 devices within the public sector programme, the assessment team noted technical weaknesses regarding prevention of infection during insertion, knowledge and skills regarding different IUD characteristics (including insertion techniques), and knowledge of the IUD's potential life span.

Experts estimated that "menstrual regulation" and abortion were increasing and that more than one million women used these methods annually.

Oral contraceptives, condoms, and vasectomy were available, but not widely accepted owing to a significant bias against these methods on the part of the providers. Also working against continued use of oral contraceptive was the misinformation that from time to time the body needed a period of rest from this method.

In general, the assessment team concluded that underutilization of methods or their inappropriate use was not due to low potential demand, but to poor quality of care and constraints within the service delivery system, exacerbated by weaknesses of the management support system.

The principal recommendation was that priority should be given to better and more appropriate utilization of fertility regulation methods currently provided in the public sector programme. The assessment team felt that Viet Nam's public health system was strong in many ways, but it still faced severe constraints. Therefore, the widespread introduction of new contraceptive technologies may burden the system further and may not improve method choice or quality of care for women.

The team recommended that the introduction of any new methods to the public sector should be handled with care and in the context of introductory research in a few selected areas prior to widespread introduction. Given the Government's interest in introducing DMPA, the team suggested that this be approached in a phased manner with introductory studies, user perspectives research and service delivery research to address the managerial requirements and service delivery adaptations necessary to introduce the method more broadly in the public sector. Such introductory research should focus on the development of strategies for strengthening of the quality of care in service delivery of all methods, rather than focusing on the introduction of DMPA alone.

Zambia

In Zambia, a participatory and "country-owned" Stage I assessment produced findings which are likely to have a major impact on future fertility regulation in the country. It was proposed that a research-based approach to the introduction of DMPA be applied in selected districts in conjunction with user perspective/service delivery research focused on the objective of improving quality of care for all methods. A need for emergency contraception also was identified. As to oral contraceptives, the Stage I assessment found that problems in the provision of this method were linked to the fact that there were too many brands of oral contraceptives on the market. As a result, the Government has moved to rationalize the number and types of the product available. The Stage I assessment also provided information for improving logistics and distribution of contraceptives, and assisted in the coordination of efforts of the various bilateral donor agencies.

Review of Stage I assessments

 A review is under way by HRP of the five Stage I assessments undertaken to date with a view to assessing the lessons learnt and to providing guidelines for countries on how to undertake such assessments. Despite the significant differences in overall contraceptive prevalence, method mix, geographical position, and political and social systems in each of the five countries in which Stage I assessments have been undertaken, all five assessments have:

● determined the need to broaden contraceptive choice;

● found that improved utilization of existing methods is of a higher priority than the introduction of new ones;

● concluded that, in general, service delivery management capability is not strong enough to introduce new methods widely

with adequate quality of care without significant change and adaptation;

● identified issues in the provision of family planning and other reproductive health services requiring policy or programme action;

● identified other research, particularly health systems research, required in reproductive health; and

● catalysed closer donor coordination.

The three underlying principles of country-ownership, participation of all stakeholders and an open, transparent process have been shown to be critical to both conduct of the assessment and acceptance of the findings for implementation. The process of bringing together policy-makers, programme managers and researchers with community and district-based providers, women's health groups, young people and the other stakeholders providing or receiving reproductive health services is not easy. These are not necessarily natural alliances nor is it normal to work across such constituencies in a collegial manner. However, it has been shown feasible in countries as different as Viet Nam and Zambia to create broad-based teams to participate in and drive activities which can result in the improvement of reproductive health care services. There is evidence that facilitation of the process by WHO staff or consultants can assist this process significantly.

The role of WHO is also important in terms of acceptance of the findings and recommendations of the report. While the product is a country report from a country-based and country-owned process, the "validation" of the conclusions from the technical perspective of WHO assists the various constituencies in acceptance of the recommendations and in planning for their follow-up.

Stage II activities

Until 1994, all Stage II activities were related to the introduction of Cyclofem, a once-a-month injectable contraceptive, into family planning programmes. The return of fertility after discontinuation of this injectable was also studied. Introductory trials have been completed during the biennium in Chile, Columbia, and Peru but as yet these countries have not decided whether or not to introduce Cyclofem.

Brazil

A Stage II research project to strengthen family planning services and to improve the use of currently underutilized methods has begun in the municipality of Santa Barbara, Sao Paulo state, Brazil. The major focus is on the operational and management changes needed to broaden contraceptive choice and provision of quality family planning and reproductive health services.

Training courses on family planning and on the early detection of cervical, uterine, and breast cancer have been offered to various health providers. A new data collection and information system has been implemented to document activities conducted at health posts, such as educational efforts, method provision, and drugs and supplies logistics. Because baseline

data demonstrated that family planning either was not addressed or had the lowest priority with health providers, a training centre and model clinic for reproductive health services was established. A key research aspect of this organizational development has been dissemination of project information. Constant contact has been maintained with officials and key community members. The community at large has been kept informed through local radio and newspapers. Plans call for the extension of this Stage II approach to other interested municipalities.

Viet Nam

In Viet Nam, a recently initiated Stage II study focuses on DMPA introduction within the context of broad method choice and improved quality of care in the provision of all family planning methods. DMPA service delivery will be introduced in two provinces, Ninh Binh in the North and Song Be in the South, while simultaneous research regarding acceptance and continuation takes place. DMPA availability will be phased in over two years until it ultimately will be available in all community health centres in four study districts.

The introduction of DMPA will be accompanied by the development of training curricula and materials, as well as IEC materials for potential users. Training will be provided to: service providers, including provincial and district level doctors, midwives, leaders of mass organizations (e.g., Viet Nam Women's Union); and community health centre personnel, community-level family planning motivators, and members of mass organizations. All fertility regulation methods will be reviewed, and emphasis will be placed on counselling, and providing balanced information as well as technical information. IEC materials for all available fertility regulation methods are being developed, as well as method-specific user information sheets to facilitate follow-up and continuity of care.

The accompanying research will investigate women's initial acceptance of DMPA, continuation rates, reasons for continuing or discontinuing, and users' perspectives on family planning (with particular reference to DMPA experiences and satisfaction, both as a method and in connection with service delivery). Also, research will focus on the technical and managerial adaptations necessary to provide improved quality of care in service delivery of DMPA and other methods.

Stage III activities

As yet no Stage III studies have been conducted under the new three-stage strategy. Moreover, planned activities with Cyclofem in Indonesia, Mexico, and Thailand were delayed owing to unforeseen developments in those countries. Indonesia did not launch Cyclofem in the public sector as per expected schedule. Mexico experienced an economic crisis. Thailand asked that the manufacturer be changed which delayed the registration of Cyclofem. There are plans for launching Stage III studies in these countries as soon as feasible.

Assuring quality of contraceptive methods

The quality of products offered by family planning programmes has a profound bearing on users' satisfaction with the products and their confidence in the services. Within the broader concept of improving the quality of reproductive health care in developing countries, HRP is developing norms and standards for quality assurance of contraceptive methods.

As the demand for contraceptive products has increased worldwide and donor contributions of contraceptive products have become more limited, a number of countries have begun, or are considering, local production. But sometimes there are problems associated with such efforts. For example, in a limited number of specimens tested, one brand of oral contraceptives produced in one country showed a range of 14%–141% of the specified content of the active hormonal agent.

Governments need information on the basic requirements for, and special considerations with regard to, contraceptive production. In 1994, HRP, in collaboration with the Program for Appropriate Technology in Health (PATH) and WHO's Division of Drug Management and Policies, prepared a document entitled "*Considerations on the production of hormonal contraceptives*", which draws attention to the regulatory, quality control, and industry structures and standards that must be in place before production of oral or injectable hormonal contraceptives should be considered.

This document is not an endorsement of local production as a solution to meeting contraceptive demands. In fact, in many cases, the importation of contraceptives will remain a more appropriate means for a country to obtain products. In countries where contraceptive production is already under way, this document can serve as a reminder of the key areas that may need to be strengthened to improve both the quality of products provided to users as well as the safety of those producing them.

HRP has also produced two other documents that will be of importance to regulatory, family planning, and industry personnel concerned with ensuring the quality of hormonal contraceptives. One is *Requirements for the quality assurance of hormonal contraceptives in family planning programmes* and the other, a companion volume, *Quality assurance of oral and injectable contraceptives—a training manual,* describes analytical methodology required to ensure appropriate quality assurance.

Understanding people's reproductive health needs and perspectives

Highlights

• Although changing slowly, attitudes favouring high fertility remain a major reason why couples in some societies do not use contraceptive methods. A study in Nigeria found that men wanted to have more children than women.

> This research emphasizes the need to include men as targets of family planning education campaigns.

• Gender roles play an important part in couples' decisions on fertility regulation. Men are often active and dominant in making decisions about fertility regulation and choice of contraceptive methods.

> Inter-spousal communication and power structure have a profound effect on how couples make decisions on fertility regulation. Planners need to consider these factors when developing services for different communities.

• Several studies reported on people's perceptions on the health effects of different contraceptive methods. Women in these studies were frequently found to report that hormonal contraceptive methods were associated with health risks.

> Family planning providers in developing countries need to be aware that many women continue to associate health risks especially with systemic methods.

• Failures of modern contraceptive methods are frequently due to ignorance about how to use the methods properly. Studies show that services often fail to meet their clients' needs.

> Both educational counselling and the organization of services need to be oriented to users' needs.

• Prospective users evaluate a number of different criteria in making their choice to use a contraceptive method. Country differences were apparent in method choice. Users who switch contraceptive methods often do so because of health concerns and side-effects.

> Users within and between countries differ markedly from one another regarding their criteria for selection of a method. Many of the reasons for discontinuing a method are amenable to intervention by improving available technologies and quality of services.

• Employment, education, urban location, land shortages, increased costs of child-rearing, and participation of women in household economic decision-making were found to be associated with lower fertility rates.

> Improvements in the status of women through their empowerment and education can help to improve their reproductive health.

HRP conducts global research on socio-cultural and service-related factors which influence reproductive health in developing countries. The aim is to help eliminate gaps in knowledge and barriers to achieving improved and sustainable reproductive health. Research on users' needs and preferences for contraceptive methods and subsequent impacts on reproductive health and fertility regulation covers, among others, the following topics:

- barriers to fertility regulation;
- the dynamics of contraceptive choice and use;
- gender roles and reproductive health;
- reproductive health of adolescents;
- sexual behaviour and reproductive health;
- determinants and consequences of induced abortion.

• Studies showed that for adolescents, knowledge about reproduction and contraceptives frequently was low or incorrect. And knowledge did not lead them automatically to practising safer sex.

The negative consequences of unwanted pregnancy, abortion, and contracting HIV/AIDS are numerous, and yet many of the adolescents studied are engaging in high-risk sexual behaviour.

• The consequences of induced abortion vary greatly between countries depending on whether abortion is legal or illegal. Where it is illegal, the procedure is carried out under unsafe conditions, with life- or health-threatening implications, accompanied often by adverse economic and social consequences. The more obvious complications of such abortions are serious infections, sepsis, haemorrhage, and sometimes death. In contrast, where abortion is legal, having an abortion (in a legitimate clinic) is a decision with minimal or no health consequences, often with very little or no expense to the woman and her family.

Every effort should be made to prevent unplanned pregnancies in order to eliminate the need for induced abortion. Depending on the legal and sociocultural conditions, each country should take appropriate steps, such as improving access to contraceptives and family planning services, to eliminate unsafe abortions.

Barriers to wider use of fertility regulation

In spite of significant increases in the prevalence of contraceptive use around the world there remain important barriers to even wider use of contraceptives. Researchers have concentrated their efforts on three main impediments to fertility regulation (not all found in each country): (i) potential users' perceptions, concerns, and fears regarding harmful effects on health associated with some contraceptive methods; (ii) poor quality of family planning services, and (iii) male dominance and opposition to some contraceptive methods.

Contraceptive methods and health concerns

People, particularly in traditional societies, are sometimes wary of modern medicine. Such suspicion also extends to modern contraceptives, especially ones that act systemically. And the fact that some methods, e.g., hormonal methods alter normal body functions such as bleeding patterns does not help. As a result researchers sometimes encounter ambivalence with regard to modern contraceptives. For example, a study in Jiangsu Province in China, based on 30 800 women, revealed a strong preference for long-acting fertility regulation methods over other supply methods, but there also was a pronounced fear of the possible side-effects of oral contraceptives.

Many newly married couples in Shanghai were apprehensive about oral contraceptives as well. Seventy-three per cent of 7800 couples were worried about oral contraceptives and 60% were unwilling to use them. Those fears included possible harm to oneself (42%) and to the couple's fetus if pregnancy occurred during oral contraceptive use (more than 33%).

A study of 725 married Turkish women in the Yapracik and Etimesgut Central areas who were using withdrawal as their contraceptive method tended to cite health concerns regarding other methods as their primary reason for using the withdrawal method. Twenty per cent of those users continued the method despite the fact that they previously had experienced an accidental pregnancy using withdrawal. Of those, 65% decided to deliver the child, while surgical abortions (29%) and self-induced abortions (5%) accounted for the remainder.

A study of Nepalese women who sought medical help due to abortion complications revealed that only 23% had been using any contraceptive method when they became pregnant. Many women expressed fears of possible side-effects of hormonal methods. In fact, use of the pill is nearly nonexistent in Nepal.

Quality of family planning services

The failure of modern contraceptive methods often may be accounted for by ignorance of users, resulting in improper use, timing errors, and so on. Sometimes users' ignorance can be traced back to poor counselling abilities of the service and method providers. Hence planners need to pay special attention to the training of service providers. Moreover, as the following example demonstrates, the services also need to be set up with the users' needs in mind.

A study of 500 Turkish women who had undergone induced abortions in two different hospitals showed that the woman's satisfaction with the two hospitals differed. Those who had been admitted to the hospital which featured integrated family planning and abortion services were more satisfied than those who were attended to by the hospital where those services were separate. And while the abortion services those women used were legal and safe, many regretted that they had not had a more individualized response to their needs. They wanted more information about the abortion procedure, as well as post-abortion counselling on family planning.

The role of men in fertility regulation

Gender relations which guide the culturally appropriate behaviour of men and women play a prescriptive role in fertility regulation in all societies. The combination of male dominance of decision-making on such issues and sometimes their opposition to fertility regulation represents an important barrier to wider use of contraception.

In Nigeria, for instance, a study focused on 92 couples using contraception and 114 couples who were non-users in order to determine what factors may have been related to the use or non-use of contraceptives. The perceived importance of the domestic roles of wife and husband, spousal communication, family decision-making, and attitudes toward contraception were analysed. Only perceptions of the domestic roles of men and

women were related to contraceptive use.

Another Nigerian study, conducted among 3073 married couples in four cities, found Nigerian men wanted more children than women did. Ninety-seven per cent of men and 91% of women agreed that men wanted more children than did women. This was especially pronounced among men with dominant views and among those who said they would depend upon their children for old-age assistance.

A study of 515 couples in Kinshasa, Zaire, demonstrated that husbands largely were in control of decisions regarding contraceptive use. A large majority of both men and women said the husband was the one who made those decisions. The study also demonstrated gender differences in the incidence of premarital sex, with nearly all the men having had sexual intercourse before marriage. However, variation among women was found. Women who were younger, who had married later, who were better educated, and whose parents were better educated were more likely to say they had engaged in sexual intercourse prior to marriage.

The dynamics of contraceptive use

There are important lessons for scientists and policy-makers in how people select, use, and discontinue use of a method. Researchers have found that there are complex factors at play in such decisions and different communities use or not use certain methods for different reasons.

Choosing a contraceptive method—motivational factors

Many factors may be considered by individuals when choosing a contraceptive method. These include: possible side-effects and health concerns, duration of protection, ease of use and of procurement, cost, effectiveness, social acceptability, reversibility, privacy, and so on. Studies showed that extremely complex motivational factors operated in contraception; that users, for example, differed markedly from one another with regard to criteria for method selection, not only between countries, but within countries as well.

The intrauterine device (IUD), for example, was selected mostly for its perceived effectiveness in India, the Republic of Korea, and Turkey, whereas its ease of use was the attracting factor among postpartum women in the Philippines. The pill was selected mainly for ease of use in India and Turkey, but for its effectiveness in the Republic of Korea. Ease of use was the major criterion for selection of depot-medroxyprogesterone acetate (DMPA) by Indian women, but the convenient duration of action was cited by women from the Republic of Korea, the Philippines, and Turkey.

That users must carefully consider a variety of factors, particularly reversibility, before choosing a contraceptive method is illustrated by a Brazilian study which found that 24% of sterilized low-income women expressed some form of regret for their decision. A Chinese study of 500 sterilized men and 500 sterilized women (compared to equal numbers of non-sterilized men and women) sug-gested that sterilization was associated with enhanced risk of depression and anxiety. However, further research will be necessary to rule out doubts about the direction of causality.

Discontinuing a contraceptive method

An estimated 42% of users of reversible contraceptive methods in developing countries discontinued the method before the end of the first year. Eleven per cent discontinued because the method failed, resulting in unintended pregnancy. Those included one in every five users of vaginal methods, periodic abstinence, and withdrawal. Only one in 14 users of the pill and injections discontinued because of failure. Another 11% discontinued because of health concerns. Those included about one in five users of the pill and injectable contraceptive methods, compared to very small percentages of users of vaginal methods (9%), periodic abstinence (0.4%), and withdrawal (0.6%). IUDs rated favourably with regard to both of those reasons for discontinuing use compared to other modern, reversible methods.

A study of 4300 women in rural areas of Hebei and Shandong Provinces, China, concerning IUD insertions found that the majority took place among the 20–29-year-old age group and among women with fewer than two children. Discontinuation of use was low during the first year (14%), but rose to 30% by the end of the third year and to 42% by the fifth year. There was a small difference in pregnancy and expulsion rates between copper and non-copper IUDs, probably because of poor insertion of copper IUDs in these rural areas.

Switching contraceptive methods

Perceived or real side-effects and health concerns associated with specific contraceptive methods (especially hormonal methods) are major contributors to users' decisions to switch contraceptive methods.

A study in the Dominican Republic examined the switching behaviour of 350 women who received hospital assistance after an illegal abortion. A review of the contraceptive methods with which the women began and the contraceptive methods to which they switched revealed that women who had used contraceptives generally began with more effective methods, then experienced problems, which resulted in their changing to less effective methods which often led to their decision to have an abortion when the latter methods failed.

Contraceptive method failure

It is generally acknowledged that vaginal methods, periodic abstinence, and withdrawal are weak contraceptive methods in terms of failure, leading to unintended pregnancy. However, more modern methods also fail from time to time, although they generally are much more reliable than traditional methods.

Contraceptive failure was studied among 1500 women who subsequently had an induced abortion in rural Sichuan Province in southwest China. Most had been using IUDs (65%), largely the stainless steel ring type which failed due to poor quality, expulsion, and other factors. Studies in China have

demonstrated that the stainless steel ring IUD method is inferior in terms of cost and benefits compared to three other methods (DMPA, Norplant, and the Copper T IUD) in urban and rural areas. For women without back or abdominal pain, the Copper T IUD used over a long period was considered cost-effective, but was inferior to DMPA and Norplant in relative cost advantages.

The empowerment of women

Several studies conducted by HRP have focused on empowerment of women in contraceptive and fertility decision-making. Those studies, broad in range, touch on many barriers and the dynamics of contraceptive use topics already enumerated.

A Kenyan study in the densely settled agricultural area of the Gussii community which had experienced land shortages focused on the relationship between women's status and fertility among three ethnic groups: the Massai, Luhya, and Abagusii. Findings indicated that several factors influenced fertility decline and demand for family planning: land shortages, increased costs of maintaining and educating children, and high unemployment (especially of women). However, the most important factor was the woman's education. Women with more education controlled family size more effectively. Further, couples whose women participated more in decision-making about household resources (especially income disposition) were more likely to achieve desired reductions in family size. However, the study noted that the traditional means of ensuring a woman's status—based on how many children she bore—was also operative and served as an alternative to education and ability to generate and control income.

Women's place in the labour force and effects on fertility and reproductive decision-making were also studied in an Argentinian project. Similar to the Kenyan study, the Argentinian study found that women who were gainfully employed had smaller family sizes compared to women who did not work for wages outside of the household. However, this effect varied according to the woman's locale. In smaller cities with traditional cultural norms, the relationship was weaker than in the large metropolitan capital of Buenos Aires, where modern mores were in force. Clearly, areas with less population had lower educational attainments and fewer employment opportunities for women, while Buenos Aires favoured early entry of unmarried women into occupational careers and also was able to absorb an influx of older women, whose families already were completed, into the work force.

In Turkey, as in Kenya and Argentina, women who worked outside the home for wages regulated their fertility more effectively and generally used more modern methods than those who stayed in the home. This was true for rural women as well as urban women (data were collected in Ankara and Van).

Although it did not examine the empowerment status of women directly, a Cameroonian study revealed findings which echoed the Kenyan, Argentinian, and Turkish results. An in-depth anthropological study of Bauieleke and Belti ethnic groups showed that urban fertility was lower than rural fertility and that the trend toward nuclear families was linked to lower fertility. Economic hardship also contributed to the desire for smaller families and increased use of contraceptives.

Reproductive health of adolescents

Success or failure among adolescents, now and in the future, will determine the course of fertility regulation in the world. Therefore, HRP has paid special research attention to this population segment.

Adolescent sexuality

A relatively high proportion of adolescents in various countries reported having had sexual intercourse. In the Republic of Korea, data from a sample of 500 single female adolescents and young adults found that 49% reported having had sex. Of these, 71% had their first experience before the age of 21 and 95% had their first experience before the age of 24.

A Chilean study found that first sexual intercourse took place between ages 14 and 17 for 51% of adolescents. In Panama, a study of 424 pregnant adolescents showed age of first intercourse to have been less than 17 years for 58% of them. A Peruvian study of 1150 night school students between 10 and 24 years of age found that 40% were sexually active; among sexually active women, 22% had their first experience before age 15. A sample of 72 women under 20 years of age requesting obstetric services at a Mexico City general hospital determined that all had become sexually active at age 15 or 16. Forty-five per cent of 400 Ugandan adolescents students sampled (aged 14–17 years) said they had experienced sexual intercourse.

A Tanzanian study found that a third of women who had submitted to an induced abortion were adolescents. Nearly half of these were 17 or younger. By age 17, more than half the women had had intercourse. Additional information regarding the length of time they had had boyfriends suggested that first sexual intercourse may have occurred at a very young age.

Relationship between knowledge and behaviour

In Indonesia, three groups were studied: adolescents, parents, and teachers. All recognized the need for conveying information to adolescents, but expressed hesitation and lack of knowledge on what to convey and how. Adolescents acknowledged their need for information, but did not know where to obtain it, despite access to sex materials. Adolescents lacked correct information and reported difficulties in communicating with parents.

For adolescents, knowledge about reproduction and contraceptives is often sparse or incorrect. Knowledge does not translate automatically into practising safe sex. Nor does lack of knowledge mean that young people will abstain from sexual intercourse.

A Mexican study uncovered a remarkable lack of knowledge about female anatomy and physiology among teenagers who were, or had been, pregnant.

Peruvian and Argentinian stud-

ies indicated that young people knew very little about sex and reproduction. Almost two-thirds of Peruvian female adolescents (64%), for example, did not know about contraceptive methods. The corresponding percentage for adolescent males was 46%. One of three males said he had used condoms, but contraceptive use among females was nearly nonexistent. By contrast, young people in Argentina had relatively high knowledge of contraception, but only 40% of the sexually active practised contraception.

Just one in four Ugandan secondary school students knew correctly when a woman is most likely to become pregnant during her menstrual cycle.

About 79% of women studied in the Republic of Korea knew about contraception, but more than 80% had not used any contraception during their first sexual experience. Many worried about becoming pregnant, but did not wish to use contraception for fear they would be labelled "bad quality girls" by their male partners. Fourteen per cent of the young women said they had contracted sexually transmitted diseases (STDs) as a result of their first coitus.

A Guatemalan study of female adolescents aged 13–19 years and their male partners (19–35 years) revealed that knowledge of condoms was almost universal among the men and very common among the females. However, they rarely used condoms. The study concluded that almost everyone had heard of acquired immunodeficiency syndrome (AIDS), but that knowledge of AIDS and other STDs generally was incorrect, with men somewhat better informed than women.

In Panama, the majority (79%) of 424 pregnant adolescent females attending for antenatal care knew some method of contraception. However, only 28% had used a method.

A Tanzanian study of 455 women with conditions relating to abortion concluded that most of the young females, aged 17 years or less, knew nothing about modern or even traditional contraceptive methods. Sociocultural norms restricted the transmission of such knowledge. School students were prohibited from using contraceptives and single women and adolescents were "not welcome" in family planning clinics.

In Chile, sexual information was not restricted. Young persons were able to obtain information on STDs through lectures, courses, brochures, posters, and books. Despite availability of information, however, they had minimal knowledge about gonorrhoea and syphilis. They were aware of the possibility of contracting AIDS, however, and expressed willingness to use condoms to prevent HIV infection.

Only half of Peruvian young adults studied were aware of AIDS and their knowledge of STDs was low. By contrast, in Kenya only 2% of a sample of 375 secondary school students had *not* heard about AIDS and 70% recommended condom use to help prevent HIV infection. The remaining students, however, felt condoms were not safe or would promote promiscuity. In Uganda, 94% of adolescents studied knew about STDs. AIDS and syphilis were mentioned most frequently and 72% had heard about methods to prevent STDs, although the quality of their information was not very high despite the fact that teachers and doctors were their two main sources of information on STDs.

Consequences of adolescent sexuality

Three major consequences of adolescent sexuality have been considered in HRP studies: pregnancy, abortion, and disease. The decision to carry a pregnancy to term or to abort was never easy and, in fact, was extremely difficult in most of the cultures studied. The decision involves a number of consequences, ranging from negative socioeconomic repercussions to adverse health consequences. A young woman may face interrupted education, undesirable marriage, social stigma, health dangers, infertility, and even death as consequences of her decision. The dangers of HIV/AIDS and STDs were ever-present for males and females, equally, if sexual intercourse was unprotected.

A Mexican study compared two groups of very young girls, one in which the girls were carrying their pregnancies to term and one in which the girls had had an abortion. Most of the pregnant girls who continued their pregnancy stopped working or studying and did not resume their studies. The girls who had had an abortion were more assertive and persistent in reaching their educational goals. Money was very important in making their decisions. A high proportion of girls decided to have an abortion but were never able to carry it out because of lack of finances and connections (abortions are illegal in Mexico). Many of those girls tried to self-induce abortion by using injections of different drugs, tea infusions, eating quinine tablets, engaging in heavy physical activity, and so on.

A Peruvian study reported that two-thirds of the pregnant adolescents studied said their pregnancies were unplanned. Fifty-three per cent did not want the pregnancy due to their young age or commitments to studies. Less than half felt happy about the pregnancy. In a study of night school students, 24% of the women who had their first intercourse before age 15 got pregnant. Almost four of every 10 pregnancies ended in abortion.

In the Republic of Korea, 58% of sexually active single respondents reported at least one abortion. Two-thirds of those abortions took place between ages 20 and 23, with an average of two or more abortions per woman. Interviews revealed that induced abortion was considered a contraceptive strategy to avoid unwanted births. Further, although abortion was legal, unsafe or unhygienic abortions seemed widespread.

In the United Republic of Tanzania, women who experienced induced abortion believed that pregnancy was the leading cause of school dropout among students. None had decided to carry their pregnancy to term, either based on their own thought processes or after receiving advice from their first confidant.

Sexual behaviour and reproductive health

This research is designed to provide baseline data on patterns of sexual behaviour in different sociocultural contexts.

Ultimately, the information will be useful to countries in development of sex education and of information and programmes for prevention of unwanted pregnancy and STDs.

High-risk behaviour of prostitutes

A study in Ghana explored the sexual behaviour of prostitutes working in Accra and Abidjan. The study demonstrated that women were dependent upon men. They had a need to supplement meagre salaries, which sometimes meant they turned to prostitution. A number of approaches to AIDS education were identified and incorporated into the national AIDS programme. Many women became motivated to use condoms and to practise safer sex.

Wife sharing and sexually transmitted diseases

One study examined the sexual behaviour of the Yagba people, a group of about two million people in Nigeria, in whom sexual sharing of wives among male kin is widely practised. Forty-one per cent of couples had suffered from STDs, 68% of them during the preceding year. Moreover, 70% reported no change in their high-risk sexual behaviour as a result of HIV/AIDS awareness. Another study in Ilorin, Nigeria, noted that male adolescents were less likely to use condoms for casual sex than for sex with their regular partner.

Acceptability of fertility regulation methods

A study completed in Viet Nam showed that both DMPA and Cyclofem were acceptable to women. Twelve month continuation rates were 75% and 77%, respectively. Focus group discussions indicated that menstrual problems were of great concern and were more often encountered among users of DMPA than of Cyclofem (81% and 47%, respectively, of discontinuations were because of serious menstrual problems).

The determinants and consequences of induced abortion

Each year an estimated 20 million women around the world undergo an unsafe abortion, induced either by persons lacking the necessary skills or in an environment lacking the minimum medical standards or both. It is estimated that of the nearly 600 000 maternal deaths each year, at least 70 000 are due to complications of induced abortion. Thus, unsafe abortion is one of the greatly neglected problems of health care in developing countries and a serious concern to women during their reproductive lives.

During the biennium, HRP completed a detailed investigation into the sociocultural factors associated with the use of induced abortions as a fertility regulation method of last resort. Research was carried out both in countries in which abortion is legal and in those where it is illegal.

Generally, where abortions were illegal, the procedure was carried out under unsafe conditions, with life- or health-threatening implications, accompanied often by economic and social ruin. The more obvious complications of such abortions were serious infec-

tions, sepsis, haemorrhage, and sometimes death.

This may be contrasted with outcomes in countries where abortions were legal. There, having an abortion was a personal decision with minimal or no health consequences, and often with very little or no expense to the woman and her family.

In Cuba, where abortion is legal, a research study found that modern contraceptives were available, but that understanding of their proper use was deficient, access was intermittent, and services, such as counselling, were inadequate. At that time, Cuba was committed to low fertility and small family sizes. The high level of induced abortion was attributed to contraceptive failure rather than non-use. Three of four women who had had an induced abortion claimed to have been using a contraceptive method in the 12 months prior to abortion.

On the other hand, a neighbouring country, the Dominican Republic, forbade abortion and had fewer contraceptive users. For instance, 56% of married women of reproductive age were users. Sterilization was the leading method (39%), followed by use of oral pills (10%). The study examined 350 women who sought hospital help due to abortion complications. Abortion was seen by those women as a last defence in the line of birth prevention methods. Three-fourths had used contraceptives in the past, but only one-fourth were using some sort of contraception at the time of their last pregnancy. Half of them were relatively new users, having used a contraceptive continuously for less than one year. Forty per cent had used contraceptives continuously for less than six months.

In Turkey, where abortion is legal, urban and rural women in Ankara and Van who had undergone a safe, hygienic abortion were questioned about their contraceptive use and abortion experience. Researchers found that 63% of married women of reproductive age used contraception, with the dominant method being withdrawal (28%). Similar percentages of withdrawal users were found in another Turkish study of 725 married women, aged 15–49 years, in Yapracik, a rural area (28%), and in Etimesgut Central, a semi-urban area (25%). Withdrawal is seen as a male method, which depends upon the male's effectiveness and motivation. Turkish men tended to prefer withdrawal, because it gave them freedom to have intercourse whenever desired and left them in control of fertility regulation. The society tended to prefer male dominance in decisions regarding fertility regulation, according to findings from both men and women among 553 couples studied in rural and urban areas. Those couples also tended to be ignorant about how modern methods worked; when they had information, it frequently was received from friends and relatives rather than from health personnel.

A third study in Turkey, conducted with 500 abortion patients in two Istanbul hospitals, involved two waves of data collection. One interview was conducted with each woman before the procedure and one was completed six months later. Like the other studies, the majority of women had depended upon with-

drawal as their contraceptive method. In their cases, it had failed. Most women reported that their husbands objected to other methods of contraception and that they had deferred to their wishes. However, withdrawal was not universally accepted by Turkish men. The Yapracik/Etimesgut Central study found that the most disliked feature of withdrawal was interference with intercourse (35% of current users) and that 12% had discontinued withdrawal because of husband's discomfort with the method. The same study revealed that women were well aware of the limitations of withdrawal as a fertility regulation method. For those who had given it up, 53% cited as their major reason the failure or fear of failure associated with it.

Taken together, the Turkish studies showed that sizeable numbers of women expressed fear of possible side-effects from modern contraceptive methods. Some women even reported that their physicians had advised against modern methods.

Nepal considers abortion a criminal act under all circumstances. A research study was carried out among women who sought hospital or clinical help in the aftermath of abortions. Contraceptive use in Nepal is very low, with only 23% of women of reproductive age using any form of fertility regulation. Sterilization is the leading method (11%). Most women said they were not using any method when they became pregnant, not even traditional methods such as withdrawal and lactation. Nearly all expressed fear of possible side-effects associated with the use of hormonal methods. Other reasons included poor access to and availability of modern methods. Nearly 90% of the women expressed interest in using a modern method in the future. Many showed a strong preference for sterilization (26%) once family size goals had been reached.

A second Nepalese study was conducted with 130 women 15 months after induced abortions. One in five reported health problems. The problems were reported more often by women whose abortions were performed by untrained rather than trained personnel (22% compared to 15%). Eighty-eight per cent had used some form of contraceptive method after their abortion, ranging from natural methods (periodic abstinence and withdrawal) (32%), oral contraceptives and condoms (20% each), female sterilization (10%), and injections (8%). At that time, 80% of non-pregnant women were using a contraceptive method, with major types consisting of natural methods (26%), condoms (18%), oral contraceptives (12%), female sterilization (12%), and injections (11%). There had been considerable method switching among users. Seventy per cent of women who were non-users planned to use contraception in the future. Eighteen per cent of the 130 women had become pregnant again. Of those pregnancies, 61% were unplanned and approximately a third were due to contraceptive failure. Seventeen per cent of those pregnancies were terminated by doctors. Sixty per cent of the sample said they would have another abortion in the event of another unplanned pregnancy.

In Mauritius, where family planning services generally were considered good, three of four married women of reproductive age used some form of contraception. Pills were the most used modern method (21%), followed by sterilization (7%). However, traditional methods accounted for 29% of the total. Abortion is illegal in Mauritius, but an estimated 10 000 or more clandestine abortions take place annually. The study concentrated on nearly 500 women who sought hospital assistance due to abortion complications. Most were married. More than half had two or more children. One-fourth had previously had an abortion. Thirty-six per cent had used misoprostol to induce their abortions. Use of misoprostol was twice the incidence of the use of herbal preparations. Researchers viewed misoprostol use as evidence that women were anxious to use what they thought was an efficient and safe "medical" option. Others had used crude methods, such as insertion of foreign objects into the uterus and carrying heavy loads. Abortion in Mauritius generally was thought of as a safety net to be used when other methods failed. Failure was due mostly to the use of traditional methods, primarily withdrawal and rhythm, and to switching from method to method. Modern methods tended to be used inconsistently.

Modern contraception availability and services are recognized as advanced in China, and abortion is legal and easily available. Two research studies, one conducted in metropolitan Shanghai and the other in rural Sichuan Province, looked at why women resort to abortion in spite easy avialability of contraceptives. Both studies found that IUD failure was the major reason women sought abortion. In

31

both studies, further examination revealed that contraceptive counselling was deficient.

The Shanghai study was undertaken to discover why married women from that city sought induced abortion at a rate twice as high as women in other Chinese Provinces (120 per thousand in 1993) and to contribute information which would lead to reduced abortion rates through the study of factors associated with repeated abortion. The sample of 2765 pregnant married women who were registered to have an abortion included rural women as well as urban women. Younger women, aged 20–24 years, and having an abortion for the first time were more likely to report they had not been using any contraceptive method at the time they became pregnant (50% and 55%, respectively). Women who reported multiple abortions were more likely to report contraception failure as the reason—85% among those coming for their third or fourth abortion, compared to 45% among women coming for their first abortion. IUD and rhythm were the most frequently cited methods which had failed. Researchers pointed to failures in Shanghai's family planning services and called for better counselling of married women.

The Sichuan Province study followed 4000 women with first trimester induced abortion at hospitals and family planning clinics in six rural counties, including remote hill areas and rice-growing plain areas. Three-fourths of abortions involved women under 30 years of age (average age, 25 years). The average number of

pregnancies among the women sampled was 1.4. Slightly less than 90% were married and only 10% had no education (as contrasted with the Shanghai study, where nearly 90% had high school or trade school educations). Of those using contraceptives, most used the IUD, which was especially popular among the young women. Older women preferred sterilization. More than half the women were seeking an induced abortion because of unintended pregnancy. Ninety per cent of those women had not been using any contraceptive method when they became pregnant. Thirty-seven per cent sought the procedure because their contraceptive method had failed. Of those, 65% used the IUD, 7% used the condom, 6% used the pill, and 22% relied on other methods.

Therefore, both Chinese studies, done in vastly different areas of the country among women with very different demographic characteristics, showed that many induced abortions were due to contraceptive method failure, mostly IUD failure.

In Mexico, a sample of 300 women was studied. They had been admitted to a Mexico City hospital for treatment of complications due to either spontaneous or induced abortion. The latter generally were conducted under poor, dangerous, and unsanitary conditions by persons who were not medically skilled (in fact, the women often performed the abortions on themselves).

Differences were found between the women admitted for spontaneous or induced abortion. Women with spontaneous abortions were more educated, had greater incomes, and enjoyed greater marital stability than women admitted as a result of complications due to induced abortions. The latter group also suffered discrimination at the hands of clinic personnel, who often were unprepared and/or loathe to treat them, even though the women sometimes were close to death. The women gave many reasons for their abortions: poverty, negative attitudes of men toward contraceptive use, preferred family size achieved, and non-use of contraceptives, whether through ignorance, fear of side-effects, or lack of motivation.

A different approach to gaining information about induced abortions was followed in a study in Sri Lanka, where abortion is illegal except to save the mother's life. There, health care providers were asked to comment on a variety of relevant topics. More than 90% saw unwanted pregnancy as a serious problem in the country. More than half said abortion incidence was "high" for unmarried women, urban women, working women, women who had involuntary sexual relations, and less educated women. On the other hand, most health providers said the incidence of self-induced abortion was "low", but that unsafe induced abortion was highly prevalent, as was safe induced abortion. More than 80% thought induced abortion was increasing. Government health institutions were said to be the main providers of post-abortion services; reasons included availability of proper medical attention, low cost to patients, and lack of services at private health institutions. The health providers supported the provision of abortion counselling for women, as well as improved sex and health education in schools and for men. Family Health Workers were viewed by more than three-fourths of the respondents as being the best coordinators for sex and health education in schools.

Expanding family planning options

Summary

• Reviews were published of the toxicological, clinical, and acceptability data on HRP's two new once-a-month injectable contraceptives, Cyclofem and Mesigyna.

Wide dissemination of these data in the scientific community is essential to build up confidence about the safety, reliability, and acceptability of these methods.

• Cyclofem is being manufactured in Indonesia and Mexico and negotiations for its possible manufacture have been completed with a major USA-based pharmaceutical company. Cyclofem has been registered in Bolivia, Guatemala, Indonesia, Mexico, Peru, and Thailand and is in the process of being registered in several other countries.

The production and registration agreements are helping to increase the use of Cyclofem in developing countries.

The commitment of HRP to expanding contraceptive options for women and men is illustrated by the fact that two of the four mission goals the Programme has set itself relate to this objective. These goals are:

• to increase informed choices in reproductive health for women by, for example, developing and testing selected methods of fertility regulation in response to women's expressed needs, at all stages of their reproductive life;
• to increase male responsibility in reproductive health by, *inter alia*, developing, testing and introducing new male methods.

• The company manufacturing Mesigyna obtained registration of the product in Argentina, Bolivia, Ecuador, Guatemala, Mexico, Paraguay and Uruguay, and began manufacturing the contraceptive in Mexico.

The increasing availability of Cyclofem and Mesigyna in Latin America is helping to expand contraceptive options for women of the region.

• In 1995, an expert review of the 1988 Bellagio Consensus on the contraceptive effectiveness of lactational amenorrhoea was sponsored by HRP, Family Health International, and the Georgetown University Institute for Reproductive Health in the light of new data that had since become available, including findings from a large HRP study on the relationship between breast-feeding patterns and the length of lactational amenorrhoea. The experts reconfirmed the validity of the 1988 Consensus.

The reconfirmation of the usefulness of lactational amenorrhoea as a method of birth spacing increases contraceptive options for women who are unable or unwilling to use other methods while they are breast-feeding their infants.

• Experts reviewed the medical eligibility criteria for the use of common contraceptive methods, and developed a classification system for the use of particular methods in the presence of specific health conditions or individual characteristics.

The new system, which is already begun to be used, should simplify the evaluation and prescription procedures for contraceptives and thus increase access to contraceptives for many women.

• WHO cosponsored a meeting of experts in Bellagio, Italy, which issued a *Consensus Statement on Emergency Contraception*, calling on family planning providers to educate themselves about emergency contraception methods and to ensure that women everywhere have access to them.

At HRP's request, the WHO Expert Committee on the Use of Essential Drugs decided to include hormonal emergency contraception in the next revision of the WHO Model List of Essential Drugs.

Availability of HRP-developed once-a-month injectable contraceptives grows

Injectable hormonal contraceptives have been in use for over 20 years. Preparations with a duration of contraceptive protection of two months (norethisterone enantate, NET-EN) and three months after a single injection (depot-medroxyprogesterone acetate, DMPA) are currently being used by more than 10 million women worldwide. Both these methods are highly effective. However, since they contain a progestogen, they cause irregularities in menstrual bleeding patterns—a factor that has limited their more widespread use.

In recent years the Programme has completed the development of two injectable preparations for use on a once-a-month schedule. Like the combined oral pills, these preparations contain a progestogen and an estrogen. This enables a great majority of users to experience a regular monthly bleeding pattern. One preparation, Cyclofem, is a combination of 25 mg medroxyprogesterone acetate and 5 mg estradiol cypionate. The other, Mesigyna, contains 50 mg norethisterone enantate and 5 mg estradiol valerate.

In early 1994, in two issues of the journal *Contraception* and in a supplement to the *Journal of obstetrics and gynecology*, comprehensive reviews of the toxicological, clinical, and acceptability data that resulted from HRP studies on these two new contraceptives were published with a view to disseminating widely the information about these two contraceptives to the international scientific and health community. Wide dissemination of these data in the scientific community is essential to build up confidence about the safety, reliability, and acceptability of these methods.

Availability of Cyclofem

Work has continued to make once-a-month injectables available to developing countries. With regard to Cyclofem, the Concept Foundation—a Bangkok-based nonprofit organization dedicated to making reproductive healh technology available to developing countries—has maintained close monitoring of the quality of the product manufactured in Indonesia and Mexico and has concluded agreements with distributors in Bolivia, Brazil, Chile, Costa Rica, the Dominican Republic, Nicaragua, El Salvador, and Trinidad and Tobago. It has continued to negotiate distribution agreements with companies in eight other Latin American countries.

Cyclofem is now registered in six countries: Bolivia, Guatemala, Indonesia, Mexico, Peru, and Thailand. During the biennium, assessments of the possible market for Cyclofem were also undertaken in Egypt, Ghana, India, Kenya, Pakistan and the Philippines. As a result, a distributor was identified in the Philippines and an introductory project will be developed in either Egypt or Kenya.

A license has been successfully negotiated with a pharmaceutical company in the USA which, if registration is obtained with the United States Food and Drug Administration (USFDA), would allow Cyclofem to be distributed through the United States Agency for International Development

(USAID). A global strategy has been developed for the distribution of Cyclofem through the affiliates of the International Planned Parenthood Federation (IPPF). Plans are being developed between the Concept Foundation and the local IPPF affiliate to make Cyclofem available in Sri Lanka.

In collaboration with the Program for Appropriate Technology in Health (PATH), field trials of Cyclofem packaged in a non-reusable injection unit, Uniject, have been completed in Brazil and the device shown to be acceptable to providers and users. Additional studies in Colombia and Indonesia are planned. It is expected that Uniject will become the preferred means of delivering injectable contraceptives in the future.

Availability of Mesigyna

Mesigyna is produced by the pharmaceutical company Schering AG. In 1995 the company began marketing the contraceptive manufactured in Mexico, and obtained registration of the product in Argentina, Bolivia, Ecuador, Guatemala, Mexico, Paraguay and Uruguay.

Lactational amenorrhoea

In August 1988 an international group of scientists gathered at the Bellagio Study and Conference Centre in Bellagio, Italy, with the support of Family Health International, HRP, and the Rockefeller Foundation. This group came to a consensus about the conditions under which breast-feeding can be used as a safe and effective method of family planning and recommended that lactational amenorrhoea should be regarded as an appropriate method of fertility regulation for many women. Studies conducted since then by various investigators have confirmed the soundness of the "Bellagio consensus" and the appropriateness of lactational amenorrhoea as a means of birth-spacing.

In 1995, experts from around the world representing fields of biomedical and social science research, family planning policy and clinical practice, medical education, and women's health gathered once again in Bellagio, Italy, to review the 1988 Bellagio Consensus. The meeting was sponsored by Family Health International, HRP, and the Georgetown University Institute for Reproductive Health. The experts reviewed the studies conducted to assess the Bellagio Consensus and reconfirmed the validity of the Consensus. Since then the three sponsors have widely disseminated the conclusions from the 1995 review meeting.

Medical eligibility criteria for contraceptive use developed

Since the 1960s, thousands of studies have been published on the safety and effectiveness of contraceptive methods. Over this period, new contraceptive methods have been introduced and methods that were being used in the 1960s have been improved. However, many of the advances that have been made in contraception have not been accompanied by updating of family planning policies and prescribing practices to reflect the progress. This has prevented the full range of methods from being available to many potential users.

In many parts of the world, family planning programmes are still being guided by policies and health care practices either based on studies of contraceptive products that are no longer widely used or on theoretical method-related health risks that have not been substantiated. In addition, international guidelines on contraceptive provision issued by various agencies and organizations have often been inconsistent and sometimes have even directly conflicted with each other. This has created confusion or has led to the perpetuation of outdated practices.

With the transition from high-dose to low-dose estrogen pills, the development of new progestogen-only methods, the widespread use of copper-releasing intra-uterine devices (IUDs) and declining use of non-medicated devices, together with the results of numerous clinical and epidemiological studies on safety and efficacy, countries now need to re-examine their guidelines for prescribing and counselling for these methods.

HRP and WHO's Division of Family Health jointly convened two meetings of experts, in March 1994 and May 1995, to redress the gap in applying recent advances in contraceptive research, to establish an international scientific consensus on contraceptive eligibility criteria, and to improve the quality of care provided in family planning services. The meetings brought together representatives of all the major organizations active in contraceptive research and programmes.

The two meetings examined the most recent scientific evidence on eligibility criteria for potential new users and continuing users of oral contraceptives, progestogen-only injectables, combined injectables, Norplant, levonorgestrel IUDs, copper-releasing IUDs, barrier methods, emergency contraception, natural family planning methods and lactational amenorrhoea. Data from more than 2000 articles published between 1985 and 1993 were reviewed.

On the basis of the scientific evidence, the experts classified the use of the above methods in the presence of specific health conditions or individual characteristics into four categories. The four categories were: (i) no prescribing restrictions required; (ii) advantages of the method generally outweigh the risks; (iii) risks usually outweigh the advantages, and therefore the method should not usually be used unless other more appropriate methods are not available or acceptable; and (iv) the method should not be prescribed at all. Each category was related to a health condition or user characteristic. So, for example, in the case of combined low-dose oral contraceptives, if a woman presents with varicose veins but is otherwise in good health, category one would be applied—i.e., there would be no prescribing restrictions. However, if a woman is less than 35 years old, is in good health, but is a smoker, category two would be applied—i.e., for her age and smoking habit low-dose oral contraceptives may be regarded to have more advantages than risks. But if a woman is over 35 and smokes less than 20 cigarettes a day, category three would be applied, meaning that the risks may be greater than the advantages. Finally, if a woman is over 35 and smokes over 20 cigarettes a day then combined low-dose oral contraceptives would be ruled entirely unsuitable for her.

The virtue of this approach is that these recommendations can be adapted to the differing situations and settings in which contraceptives are provided. Programme managers and policy-makers can consider an adaptation of the classification system when developing their service delivery guidelines. For instance, where clinical training and experience may be limited, such as in some community-based services, it may be wiser to simplify the four-category system into a two-category system. In this case, field workers such as those in community-based distribution services would generally provide a contraceptive method only if the woman falls into category one or two for the method of her choice.

A full report of the deliberations of the experts, containing the revised eligibility criteria has been prepared by WHO for wide distribution.

Emergency contraception

The last few decades of research and clinical practice have clearly established that emergency postcoital use of hormonal contraceptives is a safe and effective way of preventing unwanted pregnancy. Emergency contraception is simple and inexpensive. In most countries it can be easily made available, as it uses existing oral contraceptive formulations. Many family planning experts believe that greater use of this "last chance" or secondary method of contraception could prevent millions of unplanned pregnancies every year. But despite the important role it could

potentially play in fertility control and reproductive health, emergency contraception has yet to become incorporated into routine family planning practice around the world.

A significant obstacle to wider use in both developed and developing countries is the lack of information on the part of both women and health care providers. Because emergency hormonal contraception must be started within 72 hours of unprotected sexual intercourse, women need full knowledge of the method before unprotected intercourse occurs, and ready access to supplies once it does. Few doctors and nurses receive specific training in emergency contraception and fewer still discuss the method with patients during routine counselling on reproductive health. Also, experience from around the world indicates that the absence in most countries of products specially packaged, labelled and marketed for emergency contraception makes the regimes much more difficult to prescribe and use. The result is that while many women have heard something about a "morning after pill", most do not remember enough details about the method to take appropriate action when the need arises. Most women mistakenly believe that it needs to be taken literally the morning after. Many observers now believe that the availability of products commercially marketed for emergency contraception, with standardized instructions for health providers and their patients, would help to legitimize the method, improve correct use, and allow the method to be publicized.

In April 1995, experts from around the world, meeting in Bellagio, Italy, produced a *Consensus Statement on Emergency Contraception*, and called on family planning providers to educate themselves about the regimes and to ensure that women everywhere have access to these safe and effective ways of preventing unwanted pregnancy. The meeting was sponsored by HRP, IPPF, the Population Council, the South to South Cooperation in Reproductive Health and Family Health International, with support from the Rockefeller Foundation. One of the outcomes of the consensus meeting was the establishment of a Consortium for Emergency Contraception in which HRP participates. The other six major organizations involved in the Consortium are: The Concept Foundation, IPPF, the Pacific Institute for Women's Health, Pathfinder International, the Population Council, and PATH.

The organizations participating in the Consortium share two basic assumptions: first, that without a commercial product, packaged and labelled for emergency contraceptive use, the method's substantial potential for reducing unwanted pregnancy is unlikely to be realized; and second, that emergency contraceptive products will not be commercially successful in any country without the active support and involvement of health care providers and the family planning and women's health community. Together the seven Consortium partners offer a unique range of technical skills and international experience critical to the successful introduction of emergency contra-ceptive products, from the design of patient and provider information, to quality assurance in product manufacture. Most importantly, they can together mobilize the worldwide resources of the family planning community behind a global campaign to make emergency contraceptives an accepted part of health care for women.

Activities under the Consortium that are currently under way include the development of IEC materials for providers, users and potential users; drafting of service delivery guidelines; and negotiations with pharmaceutical companies capable and willing to produce, register and distribute a hormonal emergency contraceptive. The final choice of product—levonorgestrel or the Yuzpe regimen—will depend on the interim data from a large, 22-centre, 15-country trial comparing these two approaches which is being supported by HRP.

In response to the recommendation made at the Bellagio consensus meeting that emergency contraceptives be included in all national essential drug lists, HRP requested WHO's Expert Committee on the Use of Essential Drugs to consider including the Yuzpe regimen in WHO's Model List of Essential Drugs. The Committee, at its meeting in December 1995, decided in favour of this and hence hormonal emergency contraception will be added to the next revision of the WHO Model List of Essential Drugs.

The diaphragm

Many women's health advocates have repeatedly expressed strong support for promoting fertility regulation methods which are user-controlled, provide protection against sexually transmitted diseases (STDs) including HIV, have no (or minimal) side-effects, and foster knowledge about one's body. Specifically, one of the main recommendations has been that more research is needed on the introduction of barrier methods with emphasis on user and provider perspectives on safety, efficacy and acceptability of such methods. An interagency working group on barrier methods, comprising HRP, Family Health International, and the Population Council, has identified the diaphragm as the currently available, female-controlled method that most closely meets these criteria (except for providing proven protection against HIV).

A review of literature has revealed that there is a lack of information on the acceptability, service delivery requirements, and use-effectiveness of the diaphragm in developing country settings. The limited research available on the acceptability of the diaphragm in developing countries indicates that the percentage of women who choose diaphragms is small, but may be comparable to the number choosing other methods with a special niche like the progestogen-only pill. Lack of knowledge about

the diaphragm on the part of users and providers, the coitus-dependent nature of the method, and its relatively high failure rate may limit the number of women who will choose the diaphragm. However, the option of a "non-invasive", non-systemic method which provides some protection against upper reproductive tract infections and is associated with limited side-effects could be attractive to women who are unwilling to accept the risks and inconveniences associated with other methods.

To provide a more complete picture of the role and niche of the diaphragm in developing-country settings a three-country study (Colombia, the Philippines and Turkey) was initiated as an interagency collaborative activity. It is hoped that this study will provide initial answers to several critical questions about the potential of the diaphragm to increase contraceptive choice in developing countries. These questions include: Is there demand for the diaphragm in a free-choice environment? What are the individual and service delivery characteristics associated with successful and satisfied use of the diaphragm? What are the service delivery conditions required to provide the diaphragm with adequate quality of care?

Evaluating safety and efficacy of family planning methods

Highlights

• Combined oral contraceptive pills that contain the newer progestogens gestodene and desogestrel were shown to carry a higher risk of formation of clots in veins (deep venous thromboembolism) compared to pills that contain the older progestogens levonorgestrel and norethindrone.

> Drug regulatory authorities in some countries where pills containing gestodene and desogestrel are sold have already taken action on this finding. They have recommended improved counselling to prevent such pills from being prescribed to women who may be at a higher risk of venous thromboembolism.

HRP is committed to conducting research on the long-term assessment of fertility regulation technologies, including:

• continuing assessment of their safety and effectiveness
• post-marketing surveillance of new contraceptive drugs and devices
• interaction between methods of fertility regulation and diseases.

• Long-term use of the hormonal contraceptive DMPA (depot-medroxyprogesterone acetate) was shown not to be linked to breast cancer.

> A study concluded that DMPA should not be restricted on the grounds of breast cancer risk, but women taking it should be informed of the possibility that the contraceptive might accelerate the growth of small, existing but undetected tumours. This possibility should be considered in relation to the risks and benefits of DMPA and of other contraceptive methods. These findings led the US Food and Drug Administration to approve DMPA for use as a contraceptive in the USA.

• A study supported by HRP found that men who have had a vasectomy do not run an increased risk of cancer of the testis.

> This study, conducted in Denmark, has been valuable in allaying some of the concerns that have been raised about the safety of vasectomy. The concern about the reported association of vasectomy with prostate cancer still needs to be studied further in developing countries where vasectomy is widely used, and HRP has started a multicentre study in China, Nepal and the Republic of Korea, and is cofunding a similar study in New Zealand.

• Contraceptives containing only progestogen were shown to be safe for use by breast-feeding mothers; such methods did not affect the normal growth and development of breast-fed infants.

> This study should assure health practitioners that there is no reason to deny lactating women the use of progestogen-only contraceptives out of fear that their breast-feeding performance will be affected, or that their infants will have growth or developmental problems in the first year of life. Women wishing to use progestogen-only contraceptives do not need to stop breast-feeding.

• Results from ongoing HRP research on long-term safety and efficacy of the TCu380A IUD were instrumental in the decision by the US Food and Drug Administration to approve that IUD for continuous use of up to ten years.

> Family planning services in developing countries can offer the TCu380A not only as a birth-spacing method but also as a low-cost, highly effective long-acting method. For some women the IUD may be an alternative to sterilization.

Oral contraceptives and risk of venous thromboembolism

Combined oral contraceptives (OCs)—i.e., pills that contain an estrogen and a progestogen—were first introduced around 1960. Shortly after their introduction, case reports began to appear in medical journals suggesting that women using these pills might be at an increased risk of ischaemic stroke and thromboembolic disease. These reports were later confirmed by epidemiological studies carried out in the 1960s and the 1970s. The studies also found that the users of OCs were also at increased risk of acute myocardial infarction and ischaemic stroke, and that this risk increases if the woman smokes or has high blood pressure.

Since then, efforts to make OCs safer have led to a progressive reduction in the dosages of the two hormones in OCs (without any loss in efficacy) and to synthesis of a number of new progestogens. The reduction in the amount of hormones in OCs has been so considerable that by 1985 the amount of estrogen and progestogen in OCs had fallen to one-third and one-tenth, respectively, of their 1960s values. Also, currently some brands of OCs now contain the newer progestogens.

Concurrently with decreasing hormone dosages, another change also took place. Doctors began to prescribe OCs more carefully such that OCs are now prescribed to women with no or small risk of cardiovascular disease (e.g., younger women, those who do not smoke, and those who are not obese and do not have high blood pressure). All these factors have made it diffi-

cult to determine the extent to which changes in the dose of progestogen or estrogen and in the type of progestogen, as well as changes in prescribing practices or improved diagnostic criteria for the diseases concerned, are contributing to the apparently lower risk associated with the more recent pill formulations.

Another difficulty has been that information on cardiovascular disease risks and hormonal contraceptives, and more specifically combined OCs, has come almost exclusively from studies carried out in developed countries. Little is known about these risks in developing countries where the prevalence of risk factors and incidence rates of cardiovascular diseases are different from those found in developed countries. For these reasons HRP has regarded the further examination of the relationship between hormonal contraceptives and risk of cardiovascular disease as an area of high priority for research.

To address the above questions, a large multinational case–control study of venous thromboembolism (VTE), stroke, and myocardial infarction was conducted in 21 centres in 17 countries in Africa, Asia, Europe and Latin America. Its main aim was to determine if there was an association between currently available hormonal contraceptives and cardiovascular disease. A total of about 3800 cases of stroke, VTE, and myocardial infarction and some 11 200 matched controls took part in the study. The number of cases in the VTE group was 1143 with 2998 matched controls.

This study was completed in 1995 and two papers were published on the risk of VTE. These provided the first published observation that oral contraceptive pills containing the newer progestogens, desogestrel and gestodene, may double the risk of VTE compared with pills that contain the older progestogens, levonorgestrel and norethindrone. The other major findings published in the two papers are listed in the Box below.

Implications

Prior to publication, a summary of the results on VTE was made available to national drug regulatory authorities. Based on these results, health authorities in some countries have already taken steps they considered appropriate and have informed health care providers and users about the risks associated with pills containing desogestrel or gestodene.

HRP issued two press releases on this subject with a view to informing the general public about these findings. In the press releases, HRP experts advised that the increased risk of VTE should be interpreted keeping in mind that the incidence of venous thromboembolism in women of reproductive age is low throughout the world, and that any excess risk from using oral contraceptives affects a relatively small number of

Venous thromboembolism and oral contraceptives—main results

• The overall risk of VTE associated with oral contraceptives in the HRP study is in the lower range of the risk levels reported in previous studies.

• Women with a high body weight or those with a history of high blood pressure in pregnancy are at a slightly higher risk of VTE compared with women who do not have these problems. In the HRP study, history of hypertension or smoking habit did not alter the risk.

• Increase in the risk of VTE becomes apparent within the first months of starting the use of combined oral contraceptives and disappears within a few months of stopping their use.

• Users of combined pills that contain the newer progestogens, desogestrel or gestodene, may be at double the risk of VTE compared with users of pills that contain the older progestogens, levonorgestrel and norethindrone. This finding was quite unexpected as the two newer progestogens were thought to be safer than the older progestogens with regard to the risk of cardiovascular disease.

• It was estimated that in the United Kingdom 3–4 cases of VTE could be expected per year among 100 000 apparently healthy women of reproductive age who do not use oral contraceptives. Among women using pills containing levonorgestrel or norethindrone about 10 cases of VTE would be expected per 100 000 women per year, whereas 20 cases of VTE would occur among those who are using pills containing desogestrel or gestodene.

women. The additional risk associated with brands containing desogestrel or gestodene has been estimated to be 10 cases per year in 100 000 users over and above that observed among users of pills containing levonorgestrel or norethindrone.

Even though the use of oral contraceptive pills increases the risk of deep venous thromboembolism by some 3–4 times, the condition remains a rare event affecting only a very small number of women taking the pill. In fact, pregnancy, prolonged bed rest or immobilization, and recent surgery carry a greater risk of venous thromboembolism than oral contraceptive use.

DMPA and breast cancer

Depot-medroxyprogesterone acetate (DMPA) is administered by injection every three months and is among the most effective reversible contraceptive methods available today. It is estimated that it is currently being used by some nine million women in 90 countries. DMPA was developed in the mid-1960s with the aim of providing a reliable, reversible method that did not require taking of a pill every day. Although the injectable has been widely used worldwide, its acceptance has been influenced by concerns that it may be associated with an increased risk of breast cancer.

To study whether these concerns are justified, between 1979 and 1992 HRP conducted a large case–control study of the association between hormonal contraceptives and cancer. This study yielded vast amounts of valuable data, which

were used to build a consensus among international experts on the relationships between use of combined oral contraceptives or DMPA on the one hand and reproductive cancers in women on the other. The data from this study are now being used as a rich resource for secondary analyses and provide country-specific information on various risk factors for the cancers studied.

In 1994 HRP and the University of Otago Medical School, Dunedin, New Zealand, conducted a secondary analysis of combined data on breast cancer and DMPA which had been collected in two studies previously conducted by HRP in Kenya, Mexico, New Zealand, and Thailand. Those studies had involved 1768 women with breast cancer—most of whom were under 55 years of age—and 13 905 women who did not have the disease.

The analysis found that women using the injectable contraceptive DMPA were not at increased overall risk of breast cancer compared with women who had never used it. The study concluded, therefore, that the use of DMPA should not be restricted on grounds of breast cancer risk.

While the results confirmed the findings from previous studies, they also provided reassurance that women who have used DMPA for long periods in the past are not at an increased risk of breast cancer . However, women who started using DMPA within the previous five years appear to be at some increased risk of breast cancer (corresponding to a relative risk estimate of 2.0). But this risk was confined only to the five-year period, and women who had used DMPA more than five years previously did not show an increase in risk, even if they had used DMPA for extended periods in the past.

The reason for the increased risk of breast cancer observed in recent (or current) users could be due to enhanced detection of breast tumours in women using DMPA, or to the acceleration of the growth of pre-existing tumours.

The analysis also reconfirmed the known association of increased risks of breast cancer with early menarche, being single, late age at birth of first child, not having had any children, family history of breast cancer, and history of benign breast disease.

These results are similar to those from many studies on combined oral contraceptives and risk of breast cancer. DMPA provides high protection against unwanted pregnancy and has not been found to lead to the slight changes of blood clotting factors associated with the use of combined oral contraceptives. DMPA exerts a strong protective effect against endometrial cancer (cancer of the lining of the uterus).

Vasectomy and cancer

The relationship between vasectomy and long-term health problems or death has been studied quite extensively. Most studies have found vasectomy to be safe, and epidemiological studies of its possible consequences on health have been reassuring.

Vasectomy and prostate cancer

In 1993 two studies from the USA suggested that 20 years after vasectomy the risk of prostate cancer may increase to about two times the level of risk in non-vasectomized men. Another USA-based study also suggested a weak association between prostate cancer and vasectomy, but other studies from the United Kingdom and USA did not demonstrate any association. In 1994 a study from China also reported an increased relative risk of prostate cancer after vasectomy.

Since the findings on vasectomy and prostate cancer are conflicting, there will continue to be questions about the long-term safety of vasectomy in countries where both prostate cancer and vasectomy are common. In countries where prostate cancer is rare, the potential public health impact of any association with vasectomy is much smaller. The earlier studies that have indicated a possible link between vasectomy and prostate cancer have been conducted in the USA but the risk factors for prostate cancer are so poorly understood and the incidence so varied between countries that it is not justified to extrapolate results from the USA to other countries, particularly those with a low incidence of prostate cancer. The incidence rate of prostate cancer in the USA is 50 times higher than in some developing countries where vasectomy is prevalent, such as China.

Thus, HRP judged it to be essential that studies on prostate cancer and vasectomy are carried out in developing countries where vasectomy is widely used. Individuals who have volunteered for vasectomy are entitled to be reassured about the safety of their chosen contraceptive method. Therefore, in 1994, HRP launched a hospital-based study in China, Nepal, and the Republic of Korea and is conducting a similar study in New Zealand.

Vasectomy and testicular cancer

The findings from a historical cohort study in Denmark on the association between vasectomy and testicular and other types of cancer were published in 1994. The primary objective of this study was to find out whether vasectomy increases the risk of testicular cancer and, if it does, whether such an increase is greatest in the first years after the operation.

Contrary to indications in earlier studies, this Danish study of almost 74 000 men vasectomized between 1977 and 1989 found no link between vasectomy and testicular cancer.

Information for the study was obtained from several computerized sources: the Danish Hospital Discharge Register, the Central Population Register, the Cancer Register and the pathology registers of five Danish counties. The Hospital Discharge Register has recorded all hospital admissions and discharges in Denmark since 1977 and, since they were usually performed during a one-day admission, many vasectomies were included in this register (a sample of those performed as an outpatient service was identified from the pathology register). The Central Population Register includes information since 1968 on vital status and date of death (or emigration) for everyone in Denmark. The country's Cancer Register covers all cases of cancer diagnosed since 1943.

The study showed that vasectomized men were no more likely to have testicular cancer than were

other men. The authors concluded that it is most likely that vasectomy neither induces testicular tumorigenesis nor accelerates the growth or diagnosis of non-invasive precursor lesions or clinically unrecognized testicular cancers.

With regard to prostate cancer, the Danish study found that the risk was close to what would be expected. There was no increase in incidence associated with time after the operation, although the duration of observation after vasectomy was too short. Other studies that have collected data on the increase of prostate cancer according to time after vasectomy showed an increased risk only after around 15 years. The Danish study did not cover this period of risk and was based on few cases of prostate cancer in sterilized men (except in the older age group). Thus the authors described their findings on the risk of prostate cancer as inconclusive.

Hormonal contraceptives and effects on progeny

In many countries, the contraceptive effect of breast-feeding, more than any other method of contraception, contributes to longer intervals between births. When an infant is fully breast-fed and the mother remains amenorrhoeic, the probability of pregnancy is low during the first six months post partum. However, the risk of pregnancy among breast-feeding women increases once menstruation resumes or supplementary feeding of the infant is begun.

A large proportion of the clients in many family planning clinics are breast-feeding women. The non-hormonal methods of contraception should be the first choice for them. However, because of medical or personal reasons, many women prefer hormonal contraception, and the use of hormonal methods during breast-feeding is known to be common. Combined oral contraceptives containing estrogen and progestogen are unsuitable for breast-feeding mothers since they decrease milk output and total milk energy content. They also change milk constituents and adversely affect the duration of lactation and infant growth. Although several studies have examined the effects of progestogen-only contraceptives on lactation and infant growth, it has been difficult to interpret their results for various reasons.

Considering this issue to be important for family planning providers, HRP undertook a prospective non-randomized multicentre study to investigate the effects of commonly used progestogen-only methods on growth, development and health of infants whose mothers used such methods during lactation. The study was carried out in seven centres in Egypt, Hungary, Kenya and Thailand.

In this study, breast-feeding women requesting effective contraception were admitted at six weeks post partum. Infants of acceptors of progestogen-only methods (pill, DMPA, norethisterone enantate or Norplant implants) and non-hormonal methods (IUDs, barrier methods or sterilization) formed the study groups. Follow-up was at monthly intervals until the end of the first postpartum year.

A total of 2466 mother–infant pairs participated in the study. The mean duration of exclusive breast-feeding varied from 68 to 159 days, but did not differ significantly between study groups within centres. The mean rates of change of the anthropometric measures (weight, arm circumference and triceps skinfold) varied over time as expected, and across the centres. However, there were very few statistically significant differences in these rates of change between groups within centres. Since a large number of statistical comparisons were made, and there was no consistency either across centres, over time, or in the direction of the differences, it was concluded that, in this study, the progestogen-only contraceptives used during lactation did not adversely affect infant growth.

The component of the study related to infant development included an examination of the infant at each visit with a set of developmental tests covering gross motor, vision and fine motor, hearing, language and concept development, and self-help and social skills. The comparisons between the study groups were carried out within centres using life-table methods and Cox-model analysis with the time to first passing the test as the criterion.

There were altogether 247 comparisons between the study groups. Thirty-two (13%) of these comparisons showed statistically significant differences. In 20 instances the infants in the progestogen-only groups passed the test at an earlier age and in 12 instances at a later age, than infants in the non-hormonal groups. Since no consistent trends were observed across the centres, it was concluded that in this study the progestogen-only contraceptives used during lactation did not adversely affect infant development.

Thus, there is no apparent reason to deny lactating women the use of progestogen-only contraceptives out of fear that their breast-feeding performance will be affected, or that their infants will have growth or developmental problems in the first year of life. Women wishing to use progestogen-only contraceptives do not need to stop breast-feeding. However, to be prudent, it is recommended that contraceptive use should not be started until six weeks postpartum, as was done in this study.

Safety and efficacy of intrauterine devices

Some 110 million women, most of them living in developing countries, are currently using intrauterine devices (IUDs) to regulate their fertility. IUDs are second only to female sterilization in terms of prevalence of use.

With a view to evaluating the safety and efficacy of IUDs in developing countries and to establishing the efficacy beyond the originally approved two-year life span of the devices, HRP initiated, between 1978 and 1982, three large-scale randomized multicentre studies on three IUDs (TCu220C, TCu380A, and the Multiload) which were being introduced into family planning programmes during that period.

These ongoing studies are the largest and longest-running of their kind ever undertaken and have already yielded a rich harvest of data. On the basis of the findings of these studies the United States Food and Drug Administration (USFDA) has regularly increased the approved life span of the TCu380A from the original two years to nine years in 1993.

During the biennium the results of the tenth and eleventh years of use of the TCu220C and TCu380A were made available to the Population Council which was responsible for the original development and early testing of these devices. The Council submitted those results to the USFDA which, in 1994, approved a ten-year claim of efficacy and safety for the TCu380A. The study will be closed down in 1996 and the results published.

The usefulness of these studies for family planning services and women using the IUD has been immense. The studies recorded a cumulative pregnancy rate of 2.3 per 100 women at ten years of use with the TCu380A, which is one of the lowest pregnancy rates recorded with a reversible method of contraception. The studies have also established that for some women the IUD is an ideal birth spacing method and for some of those who have already achieved their desired family size it can be safely used as a long-term method in place of sterilization.

Developing new methods of fertility regulation

Highlights

• **Progress was made in the work to develop levonorgestrel butanoate as a new injectable hormonal contraceptive which will have a duration of action of up to three months after a single injection.**

Levonorgestrel butanoate would provide contraceptive protection for up to three months with a single 10-mg dose. Such a low-dose preparation would expose a woman to a lesser amount of synthetic hormone than is the case with depot-medroxyprogesterone acectate (DMPA)—the currently available three-monthly injectable. The lower dose would also result in less suppression of the ovaries, which in turn would result in fewer women experiencing amenorrhoea. In addition, fertility would be restored more rapidly after stopping the injections than is the case with DMPA.

HRP's mission is to increase informed choices in reproductive health for women as well as male responsibility in reproductive health. To achieve these goals, among other things, HRP:

• conducts studies to generate knowledge about mechanisms underlying reproductive processes in order to identify new research leads for the development of new, or improvement of the existing methods of fertility regulation;

• undertakes pharmacology and toxicology studies of new contraceptive methods;

• organizes clinical trials of fertility regulating drugs and devices with a view to bringing them to the market.

• **In order to meet the requirements of the United Kingdom licensing authorities for registration of the levonorgestrel-releasing vaginal ring developed by HRP, the company licenced to manufacture the rings undertook a Phase III clinical trial of machine-manufactured rings in British women.**

The study confirmed the efficacy of the ring shown in the earlier WHO studies, but also found in some women localized lesions of uncertain significance and etiology on the vaginal wall. Since pressure of the ring on the vaginal wall was a possible cause of the lesions, the ring's geometry was modified to increase its flexibility, and research is under way to assess the redesigned ring.

• **Important new knowledge was generated on the mechanism of action of progestogen-only contraceptives on the inner lining of the uterus: for example, following long-term use of Norplant the lining is rendered more prone to bleeding than is the case in a normal menstrual cycle.**

Women using hormonal methods that contain only a progestogen often complain of unpredictable vaginal bleeding. This side-effect is not only a nuisance associated with these otherwise safe and effective methods, it also adversely affects their wider acceptability and use. HRP research is aimed at developing an effective treatment for this problem.

• **A breakthrough was made in the development of a new contraceptive for men. An HRP study found that hormone injections of testosterone enantate can reduce sperm concentration in semen to either very low or undetectable levels, yielding overall contraceptive effectiveness comparable to that of the oral contraceptive pill.**

The results of this study are especially important because the development of new, safe, effective, reversible and acceptable contraceptive methods for men will expand the options available to couples who wish to plan their families. At present, the only contraceptive options available to men are the condom, withdrawal and vasectomy.

• An HRP-supported study is comparing the effectiveness and reversibility of no-scalpel vasectomy, a new chemical method of blocking the sperm ducts, and a method of plugging the ducts with medical grade polyurethane. The relative efficacies of the three procedures at 24 months after the operation, assessed by the number of men found to have a complete absence of sperm in the ejaculate, were, 98%, 99%, and 98%, respectively.

> Wider acceptability of vasectomy has been limited because of: (i) the need for a skin incision; and (ii) the difficulty of restoring fertility at a later date. The first problem has been greatly alleviated by the "no-scalpel" vasectomy procedure, in which the skin is punctured rather than cut. The development of an effective method of plugging the sperm ducts will help resolve the second problem as such a method promises to be more easily reversible.

• In an HRP study the administration of 2.5 mg or 5 mg of mifepristone (RU486) weekly did not affect ovarian function and no spotting or other side-effects were observed. But, as expected, the inner lining of the uterus was disturbed, and the effect was more pronounced with the 5-mg dose as compared to the 2.5-mg dose.

> HRP is testing the feasibility of using mifepristone as a once-a-week contraceptive pill. Research done so far suggests that it may be possible to find a dose of mifepristone that does not disturb ovulation but has a profound enough effect on the lining of the uterus to prevent pregnancy. Studies are planned to see whether the changes observed in the lining of the uterus following mifepristone treatment are sufficient to prevent pregnancy.

• An HRP study is comparing the performance of the 20-μg levonorgestrel-releasing IUD with that of the widely used TCu380A IUD. Interim analysis showed that, at 12 months of use, there were significantly higher rates of removals for medical reasons, removals for bleeding with or without pain, amenorrhoea and hormone-related reasons for the levonorgestrel-releasing device.

> A safe and effective hormone-releasing IUD is expected to produce less bleeding and pain, which are common side-effects of the copper-bearing IUDs.

• Efforts are continuing to develop a safe, effective, and acceptable immunocontraceptive that will remain effective for a predetermined period of 6, 12 or 18 months.

> Immunocontraceptives offer many potential advantages: (i) they would be free of the endocrine and metabolic side-effects associated with steroidal contraception; (ii) they would not require the insertion of an implant or device; (iii) they would be free of the storage and disposal problems of barrier methods; (iv) they could be used in a highly confidential manner; and (v) they could be produced on a large scale at low cost.

Long-acting hormonal contraception

HRP's priorities for research on long-acting systemic agents for fertility regulation focus on two products: (i) a two-to-six-monthly injectable hormonal contraceptive (using levonorgestrel butanoate); and (ii) hormone-releasing vaginal ring which has a duration of action of up to three months.

Two-to-six-monthly injectable

For several years now, HRP has been attempting to develop alternative injectable preparations which might offer significant improvements over the three-monthly injectable, depot-medroxyprogesterone acetate (DMPA). Research carried out so far has shown that levonorgestrel butanoate (a derivative of the hormonal compound levonorgestrel commonly used in hormonal contraceptives) formulated as special suspension, would provide contraceptive protection for up to three months with a single 10-mg dose. Such a low-dose preparation would expose a woman to a lesser amount of synthetic hormone than is the case with depot-medroxyprogesterone acetate (DMPA)—the currently available three-monthly injectable. The lower dose would also result in less suppression of the ovaries, which in turn would result in fewer women experiencing amenorrhoea. Also, fertility would be restored more rapidly after stopping the injections than is the case with DMPA.

Toxicity studies of levonorgestrel butanoate conducted by the US National Institutes of Health in rats and monkeys have not shown any adverse effects.

Current work focuses on testing minor modifications to the formulation in order to prevent clumping of the suspension after prolonged storage. Clinical testing in women will resume once a stable formulation has been developed. (The use of levonorgestrel butanoate in combination with an androgen preparation is also being investigated for male contraception.)

Hormone-releasing vaginal ring

Women's health advocates have argued persuasively that users need effective methods which they can control themselves. One of the major research lines supported by HRP since the 1970s has been the development of steroid-releasing vaginal rings, which would be the first long-acting method of contraception that is entirely under the control of the user. By 1985 this work had led to the development of a ring releasing 20 µg of levonorgestrel per day for a period of three months, and a licensing agreement was concluded with Roussel Laboratories Ltd. (UK) for the manufacture and distribution of this ring.

In order to meet the requirements of the United Kingdom licensing authorities for registration of the vaginal ring, the Roussel Laboratories (UK) undertook a Phase III clinical trial of machine-manufactured rings in British women. The study confirmed the efficacy of the ring observed in the earlier WHO studies, but also found in some women localized lesions of uncertain significance and origin on the vaginal wall. Since pressure of the ring on the vaginal wall was a possible cause of the lesions, the ring geometry was modified to increase its flexibility, and research is currently under way to assess the local effects of this redesigned ring.

Research on irregular vaginal bleeding from the use of hormonal contraceptives

Women using hormonal methods containing only a progestogen frequently complain of unpredictable vaginal bleeding. This is especially seen in women using long-acting methods such as DMPA and Norplant. Unpredictable bleeding is not only a nuisance associated with these otherwise safe and effective methods, it also adversely affects their wider acceptability and use.

HRP is studying this issue in three ways. First, research is under way to understand better the biological mechanisms involved in progestogen-induced bleeding. Second, HRP has developed a methodology for the statistical analysis of menstrual bleeding patterns. And thirdly, HRP is evaluating different approaches for treating progestogen-induced bleeding.

HRP research has already yielded important new concepts about the mechanism of action of Norplant on the endometrium (the inner lining of the uterus). Results have shown that, following long-term use of Norplant, there occur changes in the cells and blood vessels in the endometrium, rendering the endometrium more prone to bleeding than is the case in a normal menstrual cycle. HRP has initiated studies to explore this further.

One study is being undertaken in Bangkok, Thailand, in which two groups of Norplant users are being

compared, one with a regular bleeding pattern and the other with abnormal bleeding. The latter group is being given, in a double-blind fashion, either estradiol treatment or a placebo. The clinical effect of this treatment is being evaluated.

Another study is investigating the effects (both physiological and clinical) of estrogen treatment on progestogen-induced endometrial bleeding. In this project, Norplant users who experience breakthrough bleeding are being treated daily for three weeks with either 50 µg ethinyl estradiol (EE), a 30 µg EE-containing combined oral contraceptive, or a placebo. It is expected that data collection will be completed in 1996.

Contraceptive methods for men

The need for a wider range of methods of fertility regulation for men has been a consistent recommendation emanating from a number of international fora over the past few years including, most recently, the Fourth World Conference on Women held in Beijing, China, in September 1995. In recognition of this need the Programme has supported, since 1972, research to develop new, safe, effective, reversible and acceptable methods of fertility regulation for men as well as to monitor the safety and efficacy of existing methods.

During 1994–1995 research activities in method development continued to be focused on the three main areas of: (i) hormonal methods of inhibiting sperm production; (ii) alternative methods of blocking the sperm ducts; and (iii)

novel compounds that inhibit the fertilizing ability of sperm. This last focus has included the funding of several projects in the area of mission-oriented research on male reproductive physiology.

Hormonal contraceptives for men

The end of 1994 saw the completion of a multicentre clinical trial to assess whether severe oligozoospermia (defined as a sperm concentration in the ejaculate of 3 million per ml or less), induced by weekly injections of 200 mg testosterone enantate, equated with an acceptable level of contraceptive efficacy. The data from this study were analysed during 1995 and published in early 1996.

A total of 401 couples took part in the study which was carried out in 15 centres in nine countries. A requirement of the study was that the male partners were aged between 21 and 45 years and in a stable relationship in which both partners wanted contraception. Most of the men who volunteered for the study did so because of their, or their partner's, dissatisfaction with other methods of contraception.

No pregnancies occurred in the partners of men rendered azoospermic by the treatment and only 4 pregnancies occurred in partners of men rendered oligozoospermic. The overall pregnancy rate (1.4 per 100 person-years) is comparable with typical first-year failure rates of modern reversible female contraceptive methods, including injectable and oral hormonal contraceptives, and is far superior to the currently available reversible male methods,

i.e. condoms and withdrawal.

The average times taken to reach the required level of oligozoospermia or azoospermia (complete absence of sperm from the ejaculate) were 68 and 100 days, respectively, from the first injection. When the treatment was stopped, the average times taken for the men to return to normal fertile levels of sperm production or to reach pretreatment levels of sperm production were 112 and 201 days, respectively. All of the 33 babies born to date, to couples after they had taken part in the study, were healthy and of normal weight.

So far, the clinical studies to evaluate suppression of spermatogenesis by androgen alone have been conducted with relatively short-acting injectable preparations, such as testosterone enantate, which need to be administered every week. The acceptability of androgen injections for contraception is likely to be enhanced if longer-acting preparations were available that could be given less frequently. Indeed, the need for weekly injections was one of the drawbacks most frequently quoted by the men taking part in HRP-sponsored multicentre trials with testosterone enantate. A number of long-acting testosterone preparations are now becoming available, including: (i) natural testosterone formulated as a slow-release biodegradable implant; (ii) testosterone incorporated into sustained-release delivery systems such as the biodegradable copolymer microspheres already used successfully for the delivery of other drugs; and (iii) long-acting testosterone esters which are hydrolysed slowly in the body to release the biologically active form of testosterone over a prolonged period of time.

HRP has focused its research and development efforts on the last of these three options, in particular the long-acting ester, testosterone bucyclate. Approval to carry out the planned clinical studies with this compound has been obtained but problems have been encountered in preparing a new batch of the dosage form that meets the stringent requirements for clinical trials. Similarly, the planned clinical study to assess the ability of a progestogen-androgen combination to suppress sperm production, using the long-acting progestogen levonorgestrel butanoate and testosterone enantate, has been delayed because of formulation problems with the progestogen.

Alternative procedures to block sperm ducts (vas occlusion)

Vasectomy is one of the few contraceptive options currently available to men that has a low complication rate and a high efficacy rate. Two principal factors limit the wider acceptability of vasectomy: (i) the need for a skin incision; and (ii) the difficulty of restoring fertility if the man changes his mind later. The first problem has been greatly alleviated by the development of the "no-scalpel" vasectomy procedure (in which the skin is punctured rather than cut to reach the ducts) and this has resulted in an increased popularity of vasectomy in several parts of the world. The second problem is being addressed through the development and assessment of new devices for vas occlusion, such as silicone rubber plugs, which, if

needed, should be easier to remove subsequently to restore fertility.

A comparison of three methods of vas occlusion in China

This ten-centre study, supported by the State Family Planning Commission of China and HRP and partially funded by the United Nations Population Fund (UNFPA), is investigating the efficacy and reversibility of no-scalpel vasectomy, a chemical method of vas occlusion using methylcyanoacrylate, and a plug method of vas occlusion using medical grade polyurethane.

The relative efficacies of the three procedures at 24 months after the operation, assessed by the number of men exhibiting azoospermia, were, respectively, 98% for the no-scalpel vasectomy, 99% for the chemical (methylcyanoacrylate) method, and 98% for the polyurethane plug method of vas occlusion.

Approval of the Chinese authorities is now being sought to initiate the final stage of the project in which 5% of the men who have received each of the three procedures in all ten centres will have the sterilization reversed by microsurgery of the ducts to assess the ease of reversibility of the three procedures and the subsequent return of fertility.

Novel drugs and plant products

An ideal contraceptive drug for men would be one that neither interferes with the normal hormone balance in the body nor with the process of sperm production, but renders spermatozoa incapable of fertilizing an ovum as a result of a specific and reversible action on sperm stored in the epididymis. HRP has been in search of such a drug since its inception. Much of the work in this area in recent years has focused on the compounds isolated from *Tripterygium wilfordii*, a plant used in Chinese traditional medicine for the treatment of inflammatory conditions.

The initial clinical observations of the antifertility properties of this plant were made in China where it was found that an extract of the root appeared to have an action on sperm stored in the epididymis. Subsequent animal studies indicated that the extract may also have an action in the later stages of sperm production.

During the past biennium HRP has conducted several toxicology studies to assess the safety of the active compound isolated from the extract. No toxicity was found in these studies, some of which are still ongoing.

Non-latex condoms

HRP has developed a research protocol to determine the efficacy of new non-latex condoms in preventing pregnancy. The effectiveness of condoms when used consistently and correctly for the prevention of pregnancy and STDs including HIV is, to a large extent, established. Problems of non-use and inconsistent or incorrect use of condoms are related to their acceptability and physical characteristics. The new non-latex condoms not only offer advantages in terms of a longer shelf-life, even when stored under unfavourable conditions, but also may be better in terms of acceptability and physical properties. Acceptability has only been evaluated among

couples using other forms of contraception and there is currently no information on the comparative efficacy of the non-latex condoms compared to standard latex condoms for the prevention of pregnancy. This information is necessary to permit such new condoms to be promoted by family planning programmes and for wider use.

The proposed research is a multinational, randomized comparative trial of two types of non-latex condoms and standard latex condoms among couples using condoms as their only method of fertility regulation. Up to 3000 volunteers will be randomized to one of the three study groups and followed up at three-monthly intervals for six months (or 12 months for a subset of volunteers). The main endpoint will be the occurrence of pregnancy; a subsidiary endpoint will be the continuation rates of the three condom types used.

Contraception with the antiprogestogen mifepristone

Antiprogestogens are compounds that block the action of the hormone progesterone by binding with high affinity to the receptors for progesterone in the cells. When an antiprogestogen is administered during the phase of the menstrual cycle in which ova-containing follicles are maturing in the ovaries they disrupt the normal maturation of the follicles. Depending on how much and when the antiprogestogen is administered, the treatment can result either in demise of the dominant follicle (and emergence of a new one), or in the maturation of the follicle being arrested temporarily; the same follicle may either proceed to ovulation as soon as the influence of the antiprogestogen has passed or it may remain unruptured until the end of the cycle. It is believed that such an inhibitory effect on follicles may be a general property of antiprogestogens. This has led to the speculation that it may be feasible to develop an antiprogestogen-based, estrogen-free oral contraceptive pill. HRP is studying this approach using a sequential regimen of mifepristone followed by the progestogen, medroxyprogesterone acetate.

Since antiprogestogens block the effect of progesterone and progesterone is essential for preparing the uterus for implantation, it seemed plausible also that administration of an antiprogestogen after ovulation has occurred might have an antifertility effect. Consequently, studies were initiated by HRP to examine the effect of mifepristone, given shortly after ovulation, on ovarian function and lining of the uterus (endometrium).

When a single dose of 200 mg of mifepristone was given in the evening of the second day after the LH peak, pregnancy was prevented in the human. Also, in the rhesus monkey, a single dose of 2 mg/kg body weight of mifepristone administered a few days after ovulation prevented pregnancy. These studies suggest that the effect of mifepristone on the endometrium *per se* may be sufficient to prevent pregnancy and hence mifepristone might be used for contraception.

The suppressive effect of mifepristone on the follicles and on the endometrium are dose-related but the endometrium appears to be more sensitive to the drug. It may therefore be possible to identify a dose that does not disturb ovulation but has sufficient effect on the endometrium to prevent pregnancy. Consequently, HRP has carried out a pilot study to test the feasibility of using mifepristone as a weekly contraceptive pill. A comparable study using the compound in a low dose as a daily pill is also under way.

Administration of 2.5 mg or 5 mg of mifepristone weekly did not affect the development of follicles in the ovaries or prolong the follicular phase of the menstrual cycle. Thus, both the total length of the cycle as well as the length of the luteal phase of the cycle were unaffected. No spotting or other side-effects were noted.

The study also found that the normal development of the endometrium was disturbed following weekly administration of 5 mg of mifepristone. A similar, but less pronounced, effect was also observed following the 2.5 mg dose. Whether the changes found in the endometrium are sufficient to prevent implantation remains to be established; it is planned to conduct a small efficacy study in 1996 to determine this.

New intrauterine devices
Levonorgestrel-releasing IUD

Previous studies have shown that IUDs that release a progestogen (a compound that mimics the effect of the hormone progesterone) in the uterus are effective in preventing pregnancy and reducing menstrual blood loss. The drawback of this approach is that such IUDs have a maximum life span of 12–18 months, which is too short for most family planning programmes.

In the 1970s HRP developed and tested an IUD that released a daily dose of 2 µg of levonorgestrel (a progestogen) into the uterus. But this device was abandoned because of an excess of ectopic pregnancies. In parallel with this research, the Population Council sponsored the development and clinical testing of an IUD that releases 20 µg levonorgestrel every day. This device has been reported as having a cumulative pregnancy rate at five years of 1.1 per 100 woman–years (which indicates high efficacy), but a removal rate for amenorrhoea of nearly 20%. To date, there have been more than 70 publications on this device but very few on its performance in developing countries, where the side-effect of amenorrhoea may not be as acceptable as it is in some developed countries.

HRP's study comparing the 20-µg levonorgestrel-releasing IUD with the TCu380A started in four centres in late 1993 and in another 14 centres in 1994–1995. To date, 1414 subjects have been admitted to each of the two device groups. Interim analysis shows that, at 12 months of use, there were significantly higher rates of removals of the device for bleeding with or without pain, amenorrhoea and hormone-related reasons for the levonorgestrel-releasing device. The removals for bleeding disturbances were mainly due to irregular bleeding or spotting and to prolonged duration of menses. These findings are in line with those published elsewhere for the levonorgestrel IUD. This study is still ongoing.

Frameless IUD

Two of the major reasons for discontinuation of the use of an IUD are the side-effects of pain and bleeding and expulsion of the device. These are thought to be related to the relative size of the frame or shape of the IUD. Thus it would be expected that, if a "frameless" IUD could be inserted, these reasons for discontinuation would be minimized. The frameless IUD—the FlexiGard—consists of six copper sleeves with a surface area of 330 mm^2 crimped on to nylon suture material. The device is attached inside the uterus to the uterine wall and retained there by means of a knot in the suture material.

In a multicentre study, in which the FlexiGard device is being compared to the TCu380A, 1780 women have been recruited to the FlexiGard device group and 1690 to the TCu380A group. The pregnancy rate for the FlexiGard was significantly higher at one year of use but not at two or three years of use. The cumulative expulsion rate for the FlexiGard was significantly higher at all intervals when compared to the TCu380A but the second and third-year annualized rates were similar. The TCu380A annual pregnancy rate remains constant whereas the FlexiGard rate is highest in the first year—principally due to pregnancy occurring after an unnoticed expulsion—but thereafter, in the second and third year of use, the rates are comparable to those of the TCu380A. The provisional conclusion from this study is that the version of the FlexiGard tested by HRP, while a novel approach to the problems of expulsion and removals for pain and/or bleeding, does not fulfil the expectations of lower expulsion and removal rates because of the less than optimal inserter and insertion technique.

A modification of the inserter device and the insertion technique has been tested in nine centres supported by the International Working Group on Intrauterine Drug Delivery. The expulsion rate at three years in this study was 0.6% as was the cumulative pregnancy rate. The total medical removal rate at three years was 3.2%. These rates are very much lower than those observed in HRP-sponsored study reported above and are attributable to the improved inserter device and insertion technique.

Immunocontraception

Since 1973 HRP has been investigating the feasibility of preventing unplanned pregnancies, in a safe, effective, acceptable and non-permanent way, by immunizing against specific components of the reproductive process. The objective is to develop an immunocontraceptive that will elicit an antifertility effect for a predetermined period of six, 12 or 18 months and which: (i) will be free of the endocrine and metabolic side-effects associated with steroidal contraception; (ii) will not require the insertion of an implant or device; (iii) will be free of the storage and disposal problems of barrier methods; (iv) can be used in a highly confidential manner; and (v) can be produced at low cost.

Most of the research supported by other agencies in this area is focused on the development of immunocontraceptives which will exert their antifertility effect prior to fertilization. These preparations are intended for use by both women and men and include immunocontraceptives directed against hypothalamic and pituitary hormones which are intended to inhibit ovulation and spermatogenesis, and immunocontraceptives directed against the mature ovum and spermatozoon which are intended to interfere with gamete interaction and fertilization. Some of the anti-hormone immunocontraceptives have reached the stage of initial assessment in clinical trials but the anti-gamete immunocontraceptives are at an earlier stage of development.

To avoid duplication of effort and to ensure optimal use of the available funds, the Programme is focusing its research on the development of immunocontraceptives which will be effective after fertilization has occurred but before implantation is completed. Thus, since the mid-1970s, the Programme has concentrated its efforts on the development of an hCG immunocontraceptive based on the hCG-specific carboxy-terminal peptide of the ß-subunit of the hormone.

The Phase II clinical trial of the prototype version of this immunocontraceptive was interrupted in July 1994 following the occurrence of unexpected side-effects in the first seven volunteers to receive the preparation. As a result of detailed chemical analyses and extensive animal experiments carried out during 1995, changes

HRP's priorities in development of new methods of fertility regulation

Over the last few years, the need for the development of new fertility regulation technologies has been discussed at, *inter alia*, the International Symposium on Contraceptive Research and Development 1984–1994 (Mexico City, 1993), the International Conference on Population and Development (Cairo, 1994) and the Fourth World Conference on Women (Beijing, 1995). A review of the major recommendations and consensus reached at these fora indicates that the call for more research and development on barrier methods and new male methods has been a common theme. A meeting convened by the Rockefeller Foundation in Bellagio in 1995 on Public/Private Sector Collaboration in Contraceptive Research and Development restated these priorities and added menses-inducers to the list. Two other new elements with significant impact on the field of fertility regulation research are the increasing attention being paid to the perspectives of users and the paradigm shift from the narrow focus on family planning to the broader, holistic concept of reproductive health.

HRP needs to be responsive to changes in the expression and perception of needs for fertility regulation technologies. At the same time, HRP's budget has been decreasing and there is a need therefore to review and prioritize the research portfolio in fertility regulation technology. To this end a consultation on "Setting the agenda for research in reproductive health for the next decade: I: Fertility regulation technology" was convened in December 1995. The meeting reviewed the "products" currently under development by HRP and ranked each of them as being of high, medium or low priority based upon a set of previously agreed criteria.

Methods given high priority were:

- Mifepristone for emergency contraception
- Oral abortion regimen
- Mifepristone as a weekly pill
- Levonorgestrel butanoate as a three-monthly injectable for women
- Three-four monthly progestogen/androgen injectable for male contraception
- Mifepristone as mini-pill
- Vas occlusion with silicone plugs
- Levonorgestrel for emergency contraception
- Anti-hCG advanced prototype immunocontraceptive

have been made to the composition and formulation of the prototype preparation in an effort to eliminate or reduce the side-effects. A protocol for a Phase I clinical trial to assess the safety of the reformulated prototype has been prepared and submitted for approval to drug regulatory authorities.

Meanwhile, further studies have been carried out to assess the immunogenicity and bioneutralizing capacity of a variety of formulations of a dual-immunogen version of the advanced prototype hCG immunocontraceptive which offers the promise of a single-injection preparation with a duration of effect of six months or one year and a greater degree of effectiveness than the prototype version. Further research has also been done during the biennium to assess new hCG peptide immunogens and to investigate further the feasibility of bypassing certain steps in the immune response, as a means both to overcome genetically-determined variations in the magnitude and duration of elicited immunity and to reduce the incidence and severity of adverse side-effects, such as hypersensitivity reactions. These studies are aimed at the development of a totally-synthetic optimized hCG immunocontraceptive with the desired performance characteristics and which is easy and inexpensive to produce.

Termination of early pregnancy

Research by the Programme on the use of the antiprogestogen mifepristone for termination of early pregnancy has yielded valuable information of practical relevance. Earlier work by the Programme in this area has shown that, as a single dose, 200 mg of mifepristone appears to be the optimal amount of the drug when used in combination with prostaglandin. Higher doses of mifepristone do not increase efficacy, but efficacy starts to decline if the dose is lowered to 50 mg. Also, for optimal efficacy the nature and method of administration of the prostaglandin component of the combination is critical, especially when the length of amenorrhoea is beyond 49 days. When mifepristone is combined with one milligram of gemeprost (given vaginally) the complete abortion rate remains at approximately 95% for amenorrhoea of up to 63 days, whereas with oral misoprostol the complete abortion rate decreases with increasing length of amenorrhoea and becomes too low to be clinically acceptable in pregnancies of more than 49 days of amenorrhoea. Whether a sufficiently high level of efficacy can be maintained by administering misoprostol vaginally remains to be established.

Building capacity for reproductive health research in developing countries

Highlights

• In 1994–1995, research training grants worth some US$ 1.4 million were awarded to 90 scientists from developing countries.

> The disciplines covered by this training included biomedical and the social sciences as well as biostatistics and research management. Research training is a key component of HRP's strategy for strengthening research resources in developing countries.

• In 1995 HRP was collaborating with 54 designated WHO Collaborating Centres and about an equal number of other institutions worldwide.

> HRP's network of collaborating institutions contributes greatly to the Programme's ability to undertake multicentre research worldwide.

• Twenty-one countries in Africa and the Eastern Mediterranean region collaborated with HRP during the biennium as part of a general strategy to develop subregional centres of excellence and South-to-North links.

> This effort is in line with HRP's strategy of intensified assistance to the African region.

HRP collaborates with developing countries to identify and investigate research programmes and proposals appropriate to their reproductive health needs, and assists them in strengthening their capability to carry out research to address their own reproductive health needs. HRP shares research results with developing countries and helps them to utilize these results. Thus, HRP aims to :

• support countries in identifying priorities in reproductive health and research needs;

• strengthen the capacity of developing countries to address priority research needs and to participate in the global research effort to improve reproductive health.

• A review of research in sub-Saharan Africa showed that of the 386 reproductive health projects undertaken in 13 centres between 1990 and 1994 50% had received national funding, with the rest being funded equally by HRP and other international sources.

> HRP continues to provide significant research support in the region, which is vital to research capacity strengthening in Africa.

• Research capacity building by HRP in the Americas is bearing fruit: a review of reproductive health research carried out in the region in 1994–1995 showed that out of 263 projects in 15 centres 62% covered reproductive biology and contraception, with 40% of principal investigators being women. In 1994 HRP-supported centres published 86 papers in international journals and 74 in regional or national journals.

> HRP support has contributed to great strides being made in reproductive health research in the Americas, and the region is fast on its way to self-reliance in this field.

• An evaluation of HRP's scientific writing workshops, conducted in the Americas region between 1991 and 1994, found that the scientists who had participated in them were now publishing more research articles than they were publishing before attending the workshops.

> A total of 82 scientists in the Americas region have so far been trained in these workshops. Such training is contributing significantly to the expansion of dissemination of research findings.

• In the Asia and Pacific region, HRP is emphasizing three priorities: incorporation of women's perspectives in reproductive health research; stimulation of intraregional cooperation; and strengthening of research capabilities in the least developed countries of the region.

> Under the present strategy the least developed countries of the region are receiving up to 50% of the funds allocated to the region for strengthening research resources.

• To accelerate progress in reproductive health research by sharing knowledge and human and technical resources, to help in the creation of nationally relevant research strategies, and to contribute to individual and collective self-reliance, a series of new projects was started under the Technical Collaboration among Developing Countries (TCDC) initiative in the Asia and Pacific region.

In the Asia and Pacific region, for instance, Indonesia and Viet Nam were collaborating in a study on the determinants of fertility. Thailand was assisting the Lao People's Democratic Republic in the training of researchers as well as clinicians (in IUD insertion). In another project Thailand was also training Vietnamese clinicians in the technique of vas occlusion.

• With a view to strengthening reproductive health research in Eastern Europe, a Scientific Working Group on Reproductive Health Research in Eastern Europe was established to coordinate research and research training activities and to act as a focus for the donation and distribution of funds. The first meeting of the Group, held in May 1994, developed research proposals involving centres in Eastern Europe and a programme for research training, which have since been initiated.

Eastern Europe urgently needs to strengthen its capacity to conduct reproductive health research. Such research is needed to collect reliable information, to understand the problems and to find solutions. But both research funds and opportunities for training continue to be in short supply for scientists in the region.

Building national research capability in reproductive health

Many developing countries continue to lack both human and material resources to conduct nationally relevant research. HRP is committed to helping those countries acquire the necessary resources and enabling them to participate in the global research effort to improve reproductive health.

In undertaking activities aimed at strengthening the research capabilities of developing countries, HRP has two main objectives:

—to enable developing countries to conduct essential national research in reproductive health (as identified by the countries themselves); and

—to enable these countries, should they be willing, to participate in the worldwide research effort to improve reproductive health.

Global and regional concerns

HRP has taken up the challenge of providing necessary assistance, in accordance with the country's needs, to strengthen human resources through scientific training, to further develop facilities and to provide the equipment needed, to conduct their own national research programmes and improve their health policies and management practices. Once national capability has been built, those countries are also better able to cooperate with other developing countries and participate in global research initiatives. Thus, continuing steps are taken to ensure that developing nations have a strong voice in setting international policies in reproductive health research.

Research needs assessment

By 1994, national needs assessments, a first step in the process of research capacity strengthening, had been conducted in 17 countries by scientists, programme managers, policy-makers and others who came together, studied issues and evidence, deliberated, and set research priorities. In 1995, a critical review of the methods employed was conducted to ensure that countries would continue to have the ability to determine their research priorities and needs accurately and to stimulate innovation and experimentation in planning to meet needs and priorities.

Research training

During the biennium, continued training of research scientists was fostered through grants to 90 individuals, 51% of whom were women. Fields emphasized (as seen in the number of research training grants awarded) were andrology, epidemiology, research management, and social sciences (Table 1).

Institution strengthening

Once research needs and capacities have been determined and an institutional development plan prepared (including a statement of resources required to implement the plan), research institutions were made stronger with long-term institutional development (LID) grants and/or with recognition as a WHO Collaborating Centre for Research in Human Reproduction. In most of the latter cases there was no financial support involved in recognizing the centres beyond that needed to conduct research projects. However, a number of grants have been

Table 1. Research training grants awared during the biennium, by discipline

Andrology	12
Biochemistry	1
Clinical trials	4
Contraceptive technology	2
Epidemiology	10
Health services research	1
Laboratory techniques	3
Medical demography	1
Medical records	3
Microbiology	2
Molecular biology	5
Pharmacology	2
Public health	2
Reproductive endocrinology	5
Research management	15
Sexually transmitted diseases	4
Social science	11
Statistics	5
Toxicology	2
Total	**90**

Table 2. Designated WHO Collaborating Centres, by WHO Region, in 1995

AFRO	3
AMRO	7
EMRO	2
EURO	20
SEARO	8
WPRO	14
Total	**54**

Table 3. Institutions collaborating with HRP, by WHO Region, in 1995

AFRO	9
AMRO	20
EMRO	4
EURO	1
SEARO	16
WPRO	4
Total	**54**

awarded to develop or maintain resources.

The special attention which has been paid since 1990 to countries classified by WHO as in greatest need continued, with 14 countries receiving support: Bangladesh, Benin, Bolivia, Ethiopia, Guatemala, Mongolia, Mozambique, Myanmar, Nepal, Rwanda, Sudan, Uganda, Viet Nam, and Zambia.

Altogether, 108 institutions in 57 countries were collaborating with HRP in 1995. Half of those institutions, located in 32 countries, participated as WHO Collaborating Centres in 1995 (Table 2). The other institutions were largely in the AMRO and SEARO WHO Regions (Table 3).

World regions named for critical attention in research support

The Committee on Resources for Research, meeting in early 1994, identified three world regions for priority consideration: Eastern Europe, the Caribbean, and southern Africa. A Scientific Working Group on Reproductive Health Research in Eastern Europe was established to promote research opportunities stimulated by political and economic changes. Changes in South Africa led to the possibility of the scientific community there being integrated into global efforts and thereby strengthening other parts of Africa. Concern for the Caribbean area, expressed in an earlier Research Needs Assessment, was reiterated.

Technical Cooperation among Developing Countries (TCDC)

TCDC continues to receive high priority. Twenty projects, involving scientists from 42 countries in Africa, the Americas, and Asia, had been funded by 1995 by the TCDC initiative which is jointly funded by the Rockefeller Foundation and HRP. A priority in 1995 was the further strengthening of already established networks. Ultimately, the goal of intercountry research on common subregional issues was fostered and has developed into a major future strategy.

Africa and the Eastern Mediterranean regions

Twenty-one countries in Africa and the Eastern Mediterranean collaborated with HRP during 1994 and 1995 as part of a new general strategy to develop subregional "centres of excellence" and to promote networks through "South-to-South" and "South-to-North" links. In 1994, 29 institutional grants were awarded. In 1995, 10 institutions received LID grants and 20 others obtained assistance for resource maintenance, library support, and purchase of consumable laboratory supplies.

Under the new strategy more encouragement is being given to the improvement of research management and design of research projects, as well as training in scientific writing. The strategy to improve human resources includes emphasis on reducing internal and external brain-drain.

In the French-speaking African countries, special efforts were made to:
—stimulate interest in research on reproductive health at country level;
—disseminate research findings in French;
—create or reinforce research networks among French-speaking African scientists and institutions;
—organize regional conferences; and
—improve the infrastructure for research by developing human resources, strengthening libraries and promoting good management practices.

Activities in sub-Saharan Africa

A comprehensive review of HRPs activities in sub-Saharan Africa from 1990 through 1994 was conducted and results were presented to the June 1995 meeting of HRP's Policy and Coordination Committee. A total of 386 reproductive health research projects had been undertaken in 13 centres. More than half were supported by national funding agencies, 21% by LID and other grants and 22% by other international agencies. Some 509 publications resulted from these efforts. More than 60% were journal articles and 15% were available as congress proceedings or abstracts. A number of HRPs research initiatives had major effects on policies at the national level. Activities in selected countries are highlighted below.

Kenya. Over the years Kenya has been by far the biggest recipient of HRP funds for strengthening of research capacity in Africa. As a result, today it has well-trained scientists in various disciplines who are producing a steady flow of research results and are actively involved in human reproduction research training activities not only for Kenya but also for other African countries. The establishment of a Master's degree programme in reproductive biology during 1993 in the University of Nairobi has greatly increased Kenya's role as a regional training centre.

Mozambique. The Department of Obstetrics and Gynaecology, National University of Maputo, was awarded a first LID grant in 1989 and a second in 1994. Under the first grant the Department undertook a number of important research activities in reproductive health employing a "twinning" arrangement with the counterpart department in Uppsala University, Uppsala, Sweden. During the biennium the Department had a number of ongoing research projects in maternal health, including a study on eclampsia focusing on prevention and drug management and a study on the relationship of eclampsia to various meteorological parameters.

Nigeria. HRP's collaboration with Nigeria commenced in 1972 with the joint designation of the Departments of Chemical Pathology and of Obstetrics and Gynaecology at the University of Ibadan as a WHO Collaborating Centre for Research in Human Reproduction. Since then, collaboration has been extended to other institutions in the country.

Ongoing research at the University of Ibadan relates to: sexual behaviour of Nigerian men and women in relation to their cultural beliefs; chemoprophylaxis and pharmacotherapy of malaria in pregnant women; hormone levels and bone mass in perimenopausal women; AIDS, STDs and barrier contraceptives in young adults; and the effect on breast milk composition when depot-medroxyprogesterone acetate (DMPA) is administered to lactating women.

South Africa. South Africa possesses strong and well-equipped academic institutions. There exists a great potential for collaboration between South African institutions and HRP. In addition, South Africa could provide training for scientists from other parts of Africa, particularly in some of the specialized areas of reproductive health. Conversely, South African researchers could benefit from contact with HRP's collaborating institutions in Africa.

The return of South Africa to WHO and the potential participation in regional activities create an ideal opportunity to solicit international donor support for a programme of work aimed at fostering regional cooperation.

In May 1995, a meeting was held in Victoria Falls, Zimbabwe, bringing together seven heads of academic departments of obstetrics and gynaecology and six other key players in reproductive health research in South Africa with 16 of their colleagues from ten other sub-Saharan countries (Ethiopia, Ghana, Kenya, Malawi, Mozambique, Nigeria, Uganda, United Republic of Tanzania, Zambia and Zimbabwe) with the objective of developing mechanisms for:

—identifying research priorities in reproductive health;

—setting up collaborative research programmes;

—promoting the exchange of visiting lecturers; and

—developing exchange research opportunities within the region.

The meeting, which was jointly sponsored by the South African College of Medicine and HRP, provided an excellent opportunity for sharing information on the current status of research, research training programmes and primary health care approaches in reproductive health in countries of sub-Saharan Africa. A number of ideas were put forward on opportunities for collaboration in research and training, including the need for the production of an inventory of expertise from all countries to provide information on areas of possible collaboration. It was agreed that collaboration should be a two-way process between South Africa, on the one hand, and other countries south of the Sahara, on the other. Multicountry, multicentre research projects could arise from collaborative efforts. It was also agreed that each country should go through a national process to identify needs and set research priorities in reproductive health out of which would follow a regional priority setting and research linkages between countries.

Uganda. The Department of Obstetrics and Gynaecology, Makerere University, Kampala, was awarded a LID grant from 1989 to 1993. A second LID grant for a five-year period was awarded in 1994. Using the first LID grant to set up the basic infrastructure for research and to identify more clearly priority research needs, the Department was able to make considerable progress in restoring the research tradition which the institution enjoyed in the 1960s and 1970s. The second LID grant should enable the Department to consolidate the achievements of the first grant. The main lines of research in the Department are epidemiological studies on fertility, contraception, and maternal and perinatal health as well as clinical research on the endocrinology of infertility and contraception.

French-speaking African countries

Benin. The Centre for Research in Human Reproduction and Demography, University of Benin, Cotonou, has received a LID grant since 1987. About 40% of this grant has been spent on training a team of scientists that includes demographers, a social scientist, a microbiologist, a statistician, and an endocrinologist. In 1995, the Centre had nine ongoing research projects, most of which were supported by international funding sources other than HRP. There were no nationally funded research projects, but the staff of the Centre were often solicited to contribute to activities such as the analysis of results of studies undertaken by other local institutes and groups, the supervision of thesis work by students of various health training institutions and the delivery of lectures during various, reproductive health-related training courses.

Cameroon. The Centre for Human Reproduction Research at the Faculty of Medical and Biological Sciences of the University of Yaoundé has received a LID grant since 1987. In 1995 the Centre had 26 ongoing research projects. Eight of them were in the field of reproductive biology and 11 on maternal and infant health. The funding for 16 of the projects came from national sources, for five projects from the LID grant and for the remaining five projects from other international groups. The themes of the research ranged from effects of malaria and smoking on male reproduction to consequences of unsafely induced abortions in rural areas.

Other French-speaking African countries. Several countries developed plans for LID grant support during 1994–1995. In line with HRP's strategy for the region, the emphasis in these plans is on research training related to specific research projects that have national and regional relevance.

Eastern Mediterranean region

Egypt. In Egypt, the Department of Obstetrics and Gynaecology, University of Alexandria, was one of the earliest institutions which collaborated with HRP. It was designated a WHO Collaborating Centre for Research in Human Reproduction in 1972. HRP's institutional support to the Department ceased in 1980 when it was considered to have gone through the "strengthening" phase. This Department is an example of how HRP's long-term institutional support has enabled an institution to develop to the level where it is able to attract funds from other sources to continue its successful research programme.

A total of 59 research projects were ongoing in the Centre during 1995. Fourteen of these were in the area of contraception, 23 on maternal and infant health, 15 on infertility and seven on other areas of reproductive health.

The Centre continues to collaborate actively with different organizations within the country. In particular, it interacts closely with the National Family Planning Programme.

Also in Egypt, the Egyptian Fertility Care Society (EFCS), founded in 1974, was awarded a three-year LID grant from 1992 to 1994 with a two-year extension up to 1996. Since 1992, the Society has expanded the scope of its activities and developed its institutional

capacity considerably. During the biennium, the Society successfully completed two research projects initiated under the LID grant. One was a study of the prevalence of anaemia among Egyptian women of reproductive age and the effect of one year's use of the CuT380A IUD on haemoglobin and serum ferritin, and the other was a study of the prevalence of infertility in Egypt and its causes.

Sudan. In the Sudan, the Department of Obstetrics and Gynaecology, University of Khartoum, was awarded a LID grant in 1989. A second five-year LID grant commenced in 1994. There were seven research projects ongoing during 1995. Four of these were in the area of infertility, two on contraception and one on reproductive biology.

Tunisia. Over the last 20 years, the Centre for Research in Human Reproduction in Tunis, has received substantial support from HRP for capacity building in endocrinological research. It was in receipt of a LID grant from 1987 to 1991. In 1995, the Centre continued its participation in an HRP-supported multicentre study of "Two combination regimens of mifepristone plus misoprostol for termination of early pregnancy".

In 1995, with HRP support, the Tunisian Endocrine Society launched a new journal entitled *Revue Maghrébine d'endocrinologie-diabète et de reproduction.* This journal aims to disseminate, in French, research findings in reproductive health to the French-speaking African countries. It will also carry articles from HRP's newsletter *Progress in human reproduction research.*

Workshops and meetings in African countries

Significant intercountry workshops and meetings were held during 1994 and 1995. In 1994, these included: a sexually transmitted diseases epidemiology workshop in Harare, Zimbabwe; a scientific writing workshop in Kadoma, Zimbabwe; an epidemiological research methodology workshop for French-speaking African scientists in Libreville, Gabon; and a meeting on research needs, perspectives, and priorities for French-speaking African countries in Yaoundé, Cameroon. Also in 1994, a research needs assessment was conducted in Kenya.

In 1995 important workshops held included: an epidemiological research methodology workshop in Lomé, Togo, for 19 participants from eight countries (Benin, Côte d'Ivoire, Gabon, Guinea, Mali, Senegal, Togo, Zaire); and a scientific writing workshop for scientists from six countries (Benin, Burkina Faso, Cameroon, Côte d'Ivoire, Guinea, Senegal). An informal meeting between HRP staff and two WHO Collaborating Centres of European French-speaking countries (France, Switzerland) was also convened with the intention of increasing and integrating the involvement of these centres in HRP's strategies for French-speaking African countries.

The Americas

Three major goals were established for the Americas in 1994–1995: the establishment of regional research networks in reproductive health; provision of most research training at the regional level; and evaluation of all activities undertaken. Fifteen programme-supported centres in Argentina, Brazil, Chile, Colombia, Cuba, Guatemala, Mexico, Panama, Peru, and Venezuela operated mainly as part of four research and research training networks: reproductive biology; production of reagents for immunoassay; reproductive epidemiology and randomized trials; and social science issues in reproductive health. The last network initiated activities in 1994 and already comprises 170 researchers from 16 countries in the region, France, the United Kingdom, and the USA.

Research overview, 1994–1995

In 1994, the 15 centres conducted 263 research projects, 62% directly focused on reproductive biology and contraception. Female investigators led 40% of the projects. During 1994, investigators from these centres published 86 papers in international peer-reviewed journals and 74 in regional and national journals. They published 31 books and book chapters abroad and 43 nationally, and they wrote 190 research abstracts and official reports. They also presented 98 papers at national or regional scientific meetings and 40 at international congresses.

Follow-up research on research trainees supported by HRP between 1986 and 1994 showed that 87% of 106 grantees were back in their countries and were involved in research and research training activities in reproductive health. The multiplier effect was at work, with 4195 professional and paramedical staff trained in turn during 1994 at HRP-supported centres.

Focused regional activities

Eight Research Needs Assessment workshops were held in the region during the past five years. These workshops pinpointed national research needs, permitting the centres to become involved in projects which addressed national priorities as well as those of global interest. Examples include:

—evaluation of a single subdermal implant containing the progestogen Nestorone (ST 1435) which has a high contraceptive efficacy and few side-effects;

—development of a new system of monolithic microspheres containing progesterone and estradiol for use in long-acting contraception;

—comprehensive strategies to address the problem of maternal mortality, including the establishment of a surveillance programme, the identification of risk factors, and the demonstration of the impact of maternal deaths on family structure; and

—participation in studies to evaluate safety and efficacy of the antiprogestogen, mifepristone, in fertility regulation.

Regional and national research networks in reproductive biology, reproductive epidemiology, and social science research were strengthened:

—the network for reproductive biology fostered collaborative studies in reproductive immunology, including institutions from Argentina, Cuba, Peru, and the USA;

—the network for reproductive epidemiology, composed of centres from Argentina, Brazil, Cuba, Guatemala, and Mexico, is conducting collaborative research in reproductive health;

—a Master's degree course in reproductive epidemiology that began in Mexico in 1991 has graduated to date eight students from six countries; and

—the Center for Population Studies in Buenos Aires, Argentina, funded to lead the regional social sciences network, published its first Bulletin in 1995.

Regional reagent programmes involving Argentina, Chile, Cuba, and Mexico have been integrated in the overall plan of HRP's Laboratory Methods Group. During 1995, they developed and tested primary reagents for enzyme-immunoassay technology. This work complemented that of the Collaborating Centre in London and is part of a gradual technology transfer from the developed centre to the regional laboratories.

Three research and research training networks received HRP support for: (i) continued work in establishing resources for scientific information for regional centres, (ii) research collaboration between Argentinian and Paraguayan social scientists, and (iii) conducting a Caribbean project on maternal morbidity. Six other TCDC activities received continued funding to facilitate long-term cooperation between two or more research institutions in two or more countries.

Favourable international opinion was expressed in respect of HRP-supported centres from Argentina, Colombia, and Venezuela, which collaborated with the National Perinatal Epidemiological Unit at Oxford, United Kingdom, and with the WHO Division of Family Health in a definitive multicentre trial that compared two treatments for eclampsia. This trial was hailed by the *British medical journal* (September 1995) as a "definitive trial that signals triumph for researchers in the developing world".

Two centres from Argentina and Cuba played a leading role in preparations to implement a multicentre randomized clinical trial for evaluating a new model of

Impact of HRP's scientific writing workshops

Since 1991, in collaboration with the WHO Office of Publications, HRP has been holding workshops to help scientists in the HRP's collaborating institutions improve their skills in writing scientific papers in English and French so that they have a greater chance of having their articles published in international journals.

In 1995, to find out what participants think about the workshops some years later, and in particular to check if their training improved their ability to write scientific papers, an evaluation was conducted.

Collaborating centres in Latin America were the first to host scientific writing workshops and, by 1995, between two and four years had elapsed since a workshop had been held at those centres. This was judged to be a long enough period to allow for a meaningful evaluation of the impact of the workshops. Consequently, a questionnaire was developed and copies were sent to the centres in Argentina, Brazil, Chile, Mexico and Venezuela that had hosted the workshops. The centres were asked to get the questionnaires completed by the participants and return them to HRP. The table below gives the country and year of the workshop, number of participants, and the number of responses received.

Although the response rate was less than ideal, particularly from Chile, some 96% of the respondents said that the workshop had been useful to them. More than nine out of 10 (92%) said they were more aware of what makes a well written and well structured paper, while almost seven out of 10 (69%) said they felt more confident about their ability to write scientific papers for publication. Well over half (57%) said that the quality of their papers had improved since attending a workshop, and 53% considered themselves better able to guide junior colleagues in writing research papers. Some 43% of workshop participants felt they were able to write papers in less time than they took before, while almost half (49%) stated they could revise their papers more quickly.

The mean number of papers published in English per year before the scientific writing workshop was 1.1 and that after the workshop was 2.0. The difference was significant at p <0.001. The difference between the number of papers published before and after the workshop was significant for all the centres and was not affected by the length of research career of the participants. The questionnaires showed that 22% of the workshop participants felt they were able to get their papers published more easily than before their workshop training, and 14% said they were able to get their papers published in more prestigious journals than before.

Country and year of workshop and number of participants and responses

Country (year)	No. of participants	No. of responses
Argentina (1992)	17	10
Brazil (1993)	18	15
Chile (1991)	32	12
Mexico (1993)	15	12
Total	**82**	**49 (58%)**

antenatal care. This will be the largest controlled trial ever conducted on this topic and has attracted external funding which will enable the trial to be implemented in four collaborating institutions from developing countries (Argentina, Cuba, Saudi Arabia, and Thailand).

Renewed emphasis on the participation of women's health advocates in setting up national reproductive health programmes was fostered by a 1995 Dominican Republic meeting attended by 40 Latin American women representing a variety of perspectives, including women's health advocacy, research, policy-making, and health care provision. Recommendations from the meeting were subsequently presented to directors of the HRP's collaborating institutions in the region and to the Congress of the Latin American Association for Research in Human Reproduction. Two research proposals focusing on informed consent have been submitted to HRP by collaborative research teams from Chile and Colombia as a result of this initiative.

In-depth evaluation of strategies, activities published

Two publications evaluating HRP's activities in the region 1989 to 1993 were issued: *Expanding research capacities to improve reproductive health in the Americas* and *Research advancing reproductive health in the Americas*. A follow-up evaluation disclosed that in 1994 263 reproductive health research projects using HRP funds and assistance from other national and international sources had been conducted. While most studies

continued to focus on basic science and clinical research, 29% dealt with social science and epidemiological aspects of reproductive health—an area of growing emphasis.

Meanwhile, work continued on indicators to assess institutional development, which will facilitate evaluation of progress and comparison between institutions.

Country reports

During 1995, HRP collaborated with 22 institutions in 12 countries of Latin America and the Caribbean. Thirty-five institutional grants and three Research Training Grants were awarded. Only a few examples of these activities can be mentioned, due to limited space.

Brazil. A second five-year LID grant was awarded to the Campinas Centre for Research and Control of Maternal and Infant Disease (CEMICAMP) of the University of Campinas. This grant will focus on research and training in clinical epidemiology and social sciences related to contraceptive introduction. HRP also supports the Centre's research in male and female infertility and on the influence of hormonal contraception on cardiovascular diseases.

HRP also provided institutional support to the Centre of Reproductive Biology (CBR) in Juiz de Fora, in the form of a Resource Maintenance grant. The upgrading of the animal facilities has enabled the Centre to collaborate with other South American centres in reproductive biology using non-human primates.

Chile. Among all the countries in the Americas region, Chile has the widest range of collaborative projects in the region. Two institutions received continuing HRP support: the Chilean Institute of Reproductive Medicine (ICMER) and the Unit of Reproductive Biology and Development at the Catholic University of Chile, both in Santiago. Funding is used for training and staff support, and for major equipment purchase and maintenance. These centres also participate in HRP-supported institutional development activities in Argentina, Brazil, Panama and Peru.

Cuba. The Institute of Endocrinology in Havana has been supported by HRP in several areas. It has received Resource Maintenance grants for several years. The LID grant awarded to initiate research in reproductive immunology included support for a "twinning" programme between the Centre and the Department of Obstetrics and Gynaecology of the Harvard Medical School, Boston, MA, USA. The Centre initiated the second stage of the Reagent Production Programme, conducted in coordination with the Institute of Nutrition in Mexico, Mexico City, and the Norberto Quirno Centre for Medical Education and Clinical Investigations in Buenos Aires, Argentina. The Centre also expanded into reproductive epidemiology, and its research included a population-based study of the prevalence of STDs in pregnant women, abortion patients, and contraceptive users.

Guatemala. The Guatemalan Research Group in Reproductive Health (GRG) received HRP support to develop a reproductive health research unit for epidemiological and health service studies focused on the country's research priorities. Two areas of special GRG focus are the development of specific, Spanish-language software for perinatal and maternal mortality surveillance programmes, and the implementation of new technology to evaluate quality of care within the urban maternal and child health system.

Mexico. The Department of Reproductive Biology in the National Institute of Nutrition, Mexico City, has collaborated with HRP since 1972 and received core support until 1986. It has earned strong backing from the Government and expanded through a network of collaborating institutions to other parts of the country and region. The Department and its collaborating centres receive major support from national authorities including the Ministry of Health, which has extensive national programmes for the improvement of reproductive health. It is actively involved with the HRP's global research activities and other international funding agencies. The Department maintains a very high level of research productivity and continues to play an important role in collaboration with HRP and other research centres in the region.

Panama. The Centre for Research in Human Reproduction (CRHR), Panama City, is made up of staff from the Ministry of Health, the Faculty of Medicine, and the Social Security Hospital of Panama City. During the first LID grant period, it completed research projects in priority areas such as sickle-cell anaemia and the use of contraceptives, psychological aspects of tubal ligation, and hormonal profiles of Panamanian women.

Asia and the Pacific

More than 60% of the world's population occupies the Asia and Pacific areas. Problems are many and funds are scarce. Therefore, considerable care has been invested in HRP's activities there.

Three priorities were emphasized in these activities: (i) incorporation of women's perspectives in reproductive health research; (ii) stimulation of intraregional cooperation; and (iii) strengthening of research capabilities, especially in least developed countries.

Women's perspectives

HRP encourages participation of women scientists in establishing national research priorities, in conducting reproductive health research, in attending national and international meetings, and in disseminating research results. An especially strong women's representation was found at HRP-organized symposium session on "Reproductive Health for All: Our Common Goal" during the 15th Asian and Oceanic Congress of Obstetrics and Gynaecology in Bali, Indonesia.

Intraregional cooperation

Several projects were supported in order to promote technical collaboration among developing countries. These collaborations took the form of institutional networking or "twinning" between more advanced and relatively less advanced institutions. This approach led to the creation of collaborative research proposals and to technology transfer and sharing. Implicit goals were: to accelerate progress in reproductive health research by sharing knowledge and human and technical resources; to encourage communication between scientists; to help in the creation of nationally relevant research projects; and to contribute to individual and collective self-reliance.

Operating under these broad goals, TCDC initiatives spurred seven projects in Asia. In late 1995, five were ongoing. Each is briefly described next.

Collaboration between Indonesia and Viet Nam. A comparative study on determinants of fertility in the two countries joins the Demographic Institute, Faculty of Economics, University of Indonesia, Jakarta with the Institute for Sociology, Hanoi. Data from the Demographic and Health Survey conducted in Viet Nam are being analysed further, as the Vietnamese participants visit Indonesia to learn data analysis methods, to observe population programmes, and to do fieldwork in the countryside. Conversely, Indonesian participants have visited Viet Nam to do fieldwork.

Collaboration between the Lao People's Democratic Republic and Thailand. This collaboration is dedicated to improving health services and developing research activities in reproductive health in the Lao People's Democratic Republic (LPDR), where family planning services are not well developed and reproductive health knowledge is rather limited. The Institute of Health Research, Chulalongkorn University, Bangkok, has joined with the Maternal and Child Health Institute, Vientiane, in offering a series of workshops, courses, and other training opportunities for Lao scientists in Thailand. Topics covered through 1995 have included statistics, use of computers for data analysis, contraceptive technologies, evaluation of the birth spacing programme in LPDR (and the role of research in that programme), reproductive health and the quality of life, and STDs, including infertility. A "training for trainers" workshop was held for 20 doctors and trainers from LPDR to learn techniques for IUD insertion and removal.

Collaboration between Thailand and Viet Nam. There are three objectives of this collaboration: establish links between scientists; develop research projects related to male methods of fertility regulation, and demonstrate vas occlusion methods to the Vietnamese. Six Thai faculty offered a workshop on andrology, consisting of lectures and laboratory demonstrations, at Ho Chi Minh City, in 1995. It was attended by 23 participants and 10 observers from Viet Nam.

Collaboration between Australia and China. A twinning programme between the Shanghai Institute of Planned Parenthood Research, Shanghai, and Prince Henry's Institute of Medical Research, Melbourne, has yielded training and research opportunities for Chinese scientists, with particular emphasis on new techniques.

Collaboration network between seven countries. A workshop on "Determinants of contraceptive choice and use continuation" was conducted at the Institute of Population Research, Peking University, Beijing, China, in 1995. Particular focus was on obtaining information on reproductive health

needs and on developing a research proposal which could be undertaken jointly. Participants were from Bangladesh, China, India, Mongolia, Myanmar, Thailand, and Viet Nam. A draft proposal summarizing the rationale, objectives, methods, and expected outcome was prepared and a detailed proposal has since been submitted to HRP for evaluation and possible funding. The proposed research will target adolescents.

Strengthening research capabilities in the Asia and Pacific region

The research and managerial abilities of countries were strengthened through national and global research project support (50), consultant visits (28), Research Training grants (17), infrastructure build-up (16), workshops and courses (13), Re-entry Grants (3), and conferences/symposia (2). HRP also successfully implemented UNFPA-supported research programmes in China, the Democratic People's Republic of Korea, Indonesia, Mongolia, Nepal, and Viet Nam. UNFPA funds supported the continued build-up of staff development, research facilities, and research projects. An underlying theme throughout these activities has been the encouragement of countries to identify national priorities in reproductive health research.

Four countries have undertaken Research Needs Assessments. The process has been widely participatory and comprehensive in scope. All constituencies who provided or received reproductive health services were invited to contribute in identifying problems and in analysis. Follow-up by governments has been emphasized.

HRP has assisted in strengthening research capacities in Bangladesh, China, the Democratic People's Republic of Korea, India, Indonesia, Mongolia, Myanmar, Nepal, Sri Lanka, Thailand, and Viet Nam. A brief glimpse of a representative research effort in each country will give the flavour of this effort.

Bangladesh. The major focus in 1995 was on staff development. Four short-term Research Training grants in infertility diagnosis and management, research methods, laboratory techniques and reproductive health research were recommended. Two individuals were undergoing training; one in social science research in China and the other in epidemiology in Thailand. Limited travel to international symposia and workshops was supported. One consultant reviewed collaborative efforts between Bangladesh institutions. Research facilities were upgraded with equipment and supplies.

China. Many important ties exist between HRP and China, particularly with these institutions: the Family Planning Research Institute of Zhejiang, Hangzhou; the Shanghai Institute of Planned Parenthood Research, Shanghai; the National Evaluation Centre for the Toxicology of Fertility Regulating Drugs, Shanghai; the Division of Reproductive Endocrinology and Infertility, Department of Obstetrics and Gynaecology, Peking Union Medical College Hospital, Beijing; and the Institute of Population Research, Peking University, Beijing.

Work conducted by these institutions included research on long-acting methods of fertility regulation (particularly the development of injectable steroid preparations), synthetic and analytical chemistry, pharmacology, preclinical studies and clinical trials, large-scale epidemiological projects, and social science studies), toxicological evaluation of new drugs, studies on the behavioural and social determinants of fertility regulation, determinants of contraceptive use, fertility preference, breast-feeding and birth spacing and their relationship to infant and child mortality, and analysis of national population census data.

Democratic People's Republic of Korea. Affiliation with the Pyongyang Maternity Hospital, Pyongyang, has centred on strengthening the capability for family planning research. As the largest hospital in the country, with a well equipped section for contraceptive research, the hospital is influential in advising the Government in formulating policies appropriate for achieving the goals of the national family planning programme. Emphasis focused on expert visits, research training, strengthening of laboratory facilities, and research projects. A workshop on data management addressed biostatistics, computer applications, and research protocol design.

India. HRP has interacted intensively with these organizations: the All India Institute of Medical Sciences, New Delhi; the Institute for Research in Reproduction, Bombay; and the Indian Council of Medical Research, New Delhi. Visits were paid to the K.E.M. Hospital Research Centre, Pune; the Central Drug Research Institute, Lucknow; the National Institute of Health and Family Welfare, New Delhi; and the Safdarjung Hospital, New Delhi.

After an earlier period of intensive collaboration with Indian institutions, recent years saw a gradual decline in contacts. In 1995, therefore, a special effort was made to revitalize old contacts and to create new linkages.

Several significant avenues of cooperation have been ongoing, however, including: the development of post-ovulatory methods for fertility regulation and of methods for male fertility regulation; the identification and isolation of maturation-dependent proteins on the sperm surface and how modulation of those proteins could have antifertility effects; studies on the status of women, family planning, and fertility; and a study on the reproductive health of women in rural Gujarat.

Indonesia. Research programmes in Indonesia are coordinated through a nationwide network of multidisciplinary Human Reproduction Study Groups (HRSGs) established in medical schools. The HRSG at the University of Indonesia, Jakarta, known for its work on long-acting hormonal methods of fertility regulation, completed two major research projects in 1994. Those projects examined the etiology of increased endometrial bleeding in Norplant users, and the endometrial angiogenic response in Norplant and DMPA users. The HRSG at the Medical Faculty of Airlangga University received a LID grant for the 1992–1996 period and is embarked on an ambitious cycle of 17 research projects (eight in the social sciences, three in operations research, three clinical trials, and three epidemiological studies). The Airlangga focus is on development of basic research skills in the area of male reproduction. The HRSG at the Faculty of Medicine, Gadjah Mada University, Yogyakarta received a capital grant in 1995 and will develop special expertise in contraceptive safety, maternal and child health, infertility, and the introduction and transfer of new technologies.

Mongolia. Primary collaboration has been with the State Research Centre on Mother and Child Health and Human Reproduction, Ulaanbaatar. Research has focused on IUD efficacy, safety, and acceptability; STD epidemiology and modern microbiological techniques in the detection of STDs; and establishing normal physiological ranges of reproductive parameters. A workshop on "Infertility and infection including clinical trials in epidemiology research" was conducted for 55 participants.

Myanmar. Five institutes collaborate with HRP: the Department of Medical Research, Ministry of Health; the Institute of Medicine 1, Yangon; the Institute of Medicine 2, Yangon; the Central Women's Hospital, Yangon; and the Institute of Medicine, Mandalay. A LID grant has focused on upgrading research skills and facilities, promoting networking among participating centres, establishing mechanisms to facilitate the use of research results, and establishing a management information database in reproductive health.

Nepal. Primary institutional cooperation has been established with the Department of Community Medicine and Family Health, Institute of Medicine, Tribhuvan University, Kathmandu. Since the Department has not been very active in research in reproductive health and needed extensive assistance before it could undertake such work, a series of workshops to increase staff awareness about emerging concepts in reproductive health have been presented. Workshops also have focused on identifying a group of scientists who could be motivated to undertake research, to improve research management, and to identify research projects of direct national relevance. Research is under way on family planning and mother-child health service delivery, as well as on determinants of induced abortion and subsequent reproductive behaviour among women in three urban districts.

Sri Lanka. Sri Lankan reproductive health research is carried out by four multidisciplinary Task Forces located in Colombo, Galle, Jaffna, and Peradeniya. Coordination is accomplished through a national Coordination Committee for Research on Reproductive Health, with headquarters in Colombo. Emphasis has been on human resource development and on workshops. The workshops have focused on research proposal development, social science research methods, and data analysis.

Thailand. Strong contacts have been established with the Prince of Songkla University Faculty of Medicine in Hat Yai; the Institute for Population and Social Science Research, Mahidol University, Bangkok; and the Family Health Division, Department of Health, Ministry of Public Health, Bangkok. The Hat Yai Epidemiological Unit has developed a two-year Master's degree program and HRP has been funding scholarships for as well as supporting two research projects. Mahidol Univer-

sity has focused on family planning and STD research and also runs a Master's programmme in Population and Social Science Research, supported by HRP. A Research Training Grant was awarded to a Mahidol University student in 1995 to study applied population research at the Institute of Population Studies, University of Exeter, United Kingdom. At the Ministry of Public Health, HRP has funded LID grants in order to strengthen research capabilities to undertake research on the development of contraceptives through field trials including evaluation of the safety and efficacy of currently used methods. Workshops were conducted in 1995 on research methodology and protocol development, scientific writing and communication for scientists, policymakers and journalists. Library facilities were improved through part of the LID grant.

Viet Nam. Two institutions collaborate with HRP. The Institute for the Protection of the Mother and Newborn, Hanoi, is a tertiary-level women's hospital which provides family planning and infertility care services and acts as a resource for technical advice to the Ministry of Health and the National Committee on Population and Family Planning. HRP provides support in order to develop capabilities for research on the safety and efficacy of currently-used family planning methods and on the evaluation of new methods. The Institute issued four final study reports focusing on Vietnamese women in 1995. The topics revolved around the safety, efficacy, and acceptability of the TCu380A IUD, sterilization, and two injectable contraceptive preparations. Also, results from an epidemiological study of lower genital tract infection among Vietnamese women were released. Two staff members received Master's degree training in the fields of epidemiology and population and social science research. Two consultants visited the Institute to provide assistance with data analysis of the acceptability study of DMPA and the once-a-month injectable contraceptive Cyclofem. A workshop on protocol design and management of clinical studies was conducted for young doctors in scientific research.

At the Hung Vuong Hospital in Ho Chi Minh City, health care facilities are inadequate and modest laboratory facilities are not able to meet the demands of the clinical services. Despite these difficulties, a devoted group of researchers has emerged with ambitions to develop capacity to conduct research that supports policy-making and planning for the national family planning programme, as well as to contribute to an understanding of a variety of reproductive health problems, their causes, prevalence, treatment, and prevention. Ongoing 1995 research at the end of 1995 included a comparative trial of the TCu380A and the Multiload 375 IUDs, as well as a multicentre study comparing two regimens of mifepristone and misoprostol for termination of early pregnancy. Staff education also was continued at the Master's degree and short-term training levels.

Eastern Europe

An initiative was begun in 1990 to bring Eastern European scientists from WHO Collaborating Centres for Research in Human Reproduction together in order to assess research and service needs. Since then, two significant developments have taken place. First, a Scientific Working Group on Reproductive Health Research in Eastern Europe was established. This Group coordinates research and training activities and has developed six research proposals. Second, research training has been initiated. A postgraduate course in female reproductive health and family planning services was developed in the University of Uppsala, Sweden, in 1994. A group of Eastern European scientists also was able to participate in the annual postgraduate course for training in reproductive medicine and reproductive biology in the University of Geneva, Switzerland in 1995.

The six research proposals focus on three key problems in reproductive health in the region: family planning and contraceptive choice; health consequences of abortion; and perinatal care. Three projects are in the family planning and contraceptive choice area: the determinants of choice and use of fertility regulation methods; acceptability, side-effects, and contraceptive efficacy of long-acting injectable methods; and the preference of women seeking contraception for oral or injectable hormonal methods IUDs. Two projects are contemplated in the area of induced abortion. They will seek to provide valid data on health consequences and costs of illegal induced abortion, alleviation of those detrimental outcomes, and an examination of the impact of providing medical alternatives for pregnancy termination. In the area of perinatal care, Eastern Europe has mortality rates that far exceed those of Western

European countries. Research is needed to determine the reasons for those high rates, so that timely and appropriate interventions can be planned and implemented. Epidemiological studies are needed urgently to monitor changes in perinatal mortality and morbidity. Such studies would also provide a basis to assess the impact of environmental hazards and to monitor improvements.

Training programmes associated with proposed research programmes are contemplated.

These would focus on general and specific research management, epidemiology, reproductive health techniques, and family planning methods. Nine trainees from Romania participated in the development of a family planning manual for use in their country as part of the 1995 University of Geneva postgraduate course for training in reproductive medicine and reproductive biology.

The future of this initiative on Eastern Europe depends on continued financial support.

Adapting to meet the challenges of the future

Introduction

The Programme

The Special Programme of Research, Development and Research Training in Human Reproduction ("the Programme") was established by the World Health Organization (WHO) in 1972 to coordinate, promote, conduct and evaluate international research in human reproduction. The United Nations Development Programme (UNDP), the United Nations Population Fund (UNFPA) and the World Bank joined WHO as cosponsors of the Programme in 1988 when the World Health Assembly endorsed the role of the Programme in 'coordination of the global research effort in the field of reproductive health'. As the main instrument within the United Nations system for research in human reproduction, the Programme brings together health care providers, policy-makers, scientists, clinicians and the community to identify priorities for research and for the strengthening, in developing countries, of research institutions.

For much of the life of the Programme, priorities have included research on new methods of fertility regulation for both women and men, on the introduction of methods to family planning programmes, on the long-term safety of methods already in use and other aspects of epidemiological research in repro-

ductive health, on social and behavioural aspects of reproductive health, and on methods of controlling the spread of sexually transmitted diseases which can cause infertility. The Programme also carries out activities to strengthen the research capabilities of developing countries to enable them to meet their own research needs and participate in the global effort in human reproduction research.

Reproductive health

WHO's technical definition of reproductive health was adopted with minor modifications (see box on next page) by the International Conference on Population and Development (ICPD), held in Cairo in September 1994, and was included in the Programme of Action arising from the Conference.

The commitment

The ICPD Programme of Action acknowledged reproductive health as a cornerstone of health. It also called for an increased commitment to and support for reproductive health research and requested WHO to continue to provide, at the request of countries, advice on family planning methods. More specifically the ICPD called for:

—reliable information on issues of safety and effectiveness of fertility regulating methods;

—an intensified effort in biomedical

and social science research that will enable men to take a greater responsibility for reproductive health; and

—research to develop methods that can be controlled by users and

research problems in reproductive health. Through its own consultative mechanisms, the Programme has already established a research agenda that reflects these needs.

The mandate

In recent years the Programme has responded to the changing environment of reproductive health and has, at the request of its governing body, the Policy and Coordination Committee (PCC), positioned its activities in fertility regulation in a wider reproductive health context. In June 1993, the PCC agreed to initiate a review of the Programme's mandate in the context of WHO's overall role in reproductive health. Since then the Programme has defined the recasting of its strategic focus taking account of developments in the understanding of reproductive health and the Programme's comparative strengths and those of other organizations and agencies working in the field.

The mandate was agreed in 1995 as follows:

"Within the framework of the global strategy for reproductive health, and with particular reference to the needs of individuals and couples in developing countries, the UNDP/UNFPA/WHO/World Bank Special Programme of Research, Development and Research Training in Human Reproduction is the main instrument within the United Nations system for promoting, conducting, evaluating and coordinating interdisciplinary research on reproductive health, for collaborating with countries in enhancing national capacities to conduct such research, for

---

Definition of reproductive health

Reproductive health is a state of complete physical, mental and social well-being and not merely the absence of disease or infirmity, in all matters relating to the reproductive system and to its functions and processes. Reproductive health therefore implies that people are able to have a satisfying and safe sex life and that they have the capability to reproduce and the freedom to decide if, when and how often to do so. Implicit in this last condition are the right of men and women to be informed and to have access to safe, effective, affordable and acceptable methods of family planning of their choice, as well as other methods of their choice for regulation of fertility which are not against the law, and the right of access to appropriate health-care services that will enable women to go safely through pregnancy and childbirth and provide couples with the best chance of having a healthy infant. In line with the above definition of reproductive health, reproductive health care is defined as the constellation of methods, techniques and services that contribute to reproductive health and well-being by preventing and solving reproductive health problems. It also includes sexual health, the purpose of which is the enhancement of life and personal relations, and not merely counselling and care related to reproduction and sexually transmitted diseases."

---

which can provide protection against sexually transmitted diseases(STDs) including human immunodeficiency virus/acquired immune deficiency syndrome(HIV/AIDS).

The ICPD recognized the importance of a careful assessment of existing service infrastructure, user needs and preferences, and other factors that influence activities to broaden contraceptive choice and importance of efforts to enhance the capability of developing countries to address their own promoting the use of research results in policy-making and planning for reproductive health care at national and international levels, and for the setting of standards and guidelines, including ethical guidelines, in the field of reproductive health research."

The Programme's comparative advantages

The Programme exists in an environment shaped by the numerous needs and requirements of:
—individuals and couples;
—governments, regulatory agencies, policy-makers, non-governmental organizations, family planning programme managers, service providers;
—research scientists and institutions;
—women's health advocacy groups;
—consumer groups;
—cosponsors and donors, bilateral and multilateral development agencies; and
—the pharmaceutical industry.

As a cosponsored programme executed by the World Health Organization, the Programme:
—has the mandate to provide guidance to Member States on technical and ethical issues in reproductive health;
—benefits from extensive mechanisms for consultation with developing countries;
—is the only agency offering comprehensive technical assistance for institutional development based on the identification of national research priorities in reproductive health;
—has immediate access to a broad range of expertise in public health;

—is able to attract international expertise at relatively low cost; and
—attracts matching funds from the countries in which activities take place.

In establishing its research agenda, the Programme has:
—a commitment to the assessment of the long-term safety and effectiveness of methods of fertility regulation in both developed and developing country settings.
—the ability to integrate social science research with method development, reflecting sensitivity to different cultures and service settings; and
—the independence to conduct research on sensitive issues such as abortion and sexual behaviour.

With more than twenty years' experience in multidisciplinary reproductive health research, the Programme has:
—an established record of success in developing national resources for basic research, product development and clinical testing and in facilitating participation of developing countries in the global research effort;
—access to its proven and effective international network of clinical, epidemiological and social science research institutes;
—the ability to negotiate with industry preferential public sector pricing structures for family planning programmes in developing countries.

These comparative advantages highlight the unique nature of the Programme and its ability to respond to its external environment. There is no other organization that has the scientific integrity, objectivity and independence of the Programme in the field of fertility regulation. The products and servi-

Vision

The Programme shall provide leadership in international reproductive health research.

The Programme shall pursue a dynamic research strategy sensitive to people's changing needs.

The Programme shall generate and disseminate knowledge and technologies aimed at reducing inequities in reproductive health.

The Programme shall promote self-reliance in reproductive health research in developing countries.

ces provided by the Programme have been developed through the work of its staff in collaboration with a worldwide network of scientists and under the guidance of its technical and advisory bodies over a period of more than two decades. It has well established mechanisms for conducting research and for strengthening research capabilities. Moreover, because it is based within WHO, Member States look to the Programme to provide unbiased, technically sound advice and assistance and to work with developing countries to determine and address countries' needs.

The strategic focus of the Programme

While the Programme's broad mandate places its activities within the overall concept of reproductive health, in the current period of financial constraint, the Programme will continue to focus its work in the area where it has a strong comparative advantage, namely fertility regulation. Access, at the primary health care level, to safe, acceptable, effective and appropriate methods of regulating fertility is central to many other aspects of reproductive health and will make a significant contribution to improving the health of women and men. Research gathers the reliable information needed to make this possible.

Programme staff have since late 1993 defined the Programme's Vision and have made a clear statement on its future Mission Goals in terms of the broad mandate and focused mission.

Understanding the challenges to reproductive health research

The challenges and tasks needing scientific investigation and the manner in which the Programme's activities interrelate in bringing about beneficial change in reproductive health are illustrated in Fig. 1. This is a conceptual model which points to three broad areas to which the Programme contributes and which indicates the Programme's activities in each.

The first area comprises a situation analysis which involves the review of reproductive health in a country, regionally or even globally, in order to identify problems and the issues which merit priority attention. The second area covers research to develop new technologies and methodologies that can be brought to bear on the problems identified, to gather information and to establish norms. The third area is concerned with the application of new technologies and information together with the long-term assessment of the health consequences of technologies and the evaluation of the health and social impact of the Programme's initiatives. These three areas are considered in more detail below. Situation analysis can lead directly to introduction and evaluation with passage through technology development as required.

Throughout this process, every effort is made to ensure the full participation of women in the setting of the research agenda and their continued involvement in all subsequent activities, by promoting and sustaining a dialogue with women's health advocates and membership of women in technical advisory committees of the Programme.

Situation analysis

It is in the area of situation analysis that the Programme has the maximum opportunity and responsibility to collaborate with complementary programmes, both within and outside WHO, in undertaking a comprehensive assessment that will underpin WHO's reproductive health strategy. Since activities undertaken by the Programme may identify problems that fall outside its strategic focus or even its mandate, a special effort is made to disseminate and to actively share information so that others may respond.

The Programme draws upon the regional expertise of developing country nationals who participate in the Programme's policy, advisory and technical committees. At country level the Programme uses three broad approaches to the analysis of the situation which lead to identification of the most appropriate course of action.

- *Reproductive health assessment*
  The Programme, together with other relevant WHO programmes, encourages and facilitates the comprehensive assessment of reproductive health needs. This is a participatory process that involves representatives of all those who are providing or receiving reproductive health care.

- *Collaborative research activities*
  —the nature and extent of reproductive health problems;
  —the risk factors associated with these problems;
  —user needs and preferences, contraceptive use dynamics;
  —gender roles and reproductive

Fig. 1. The process of reproductive health research

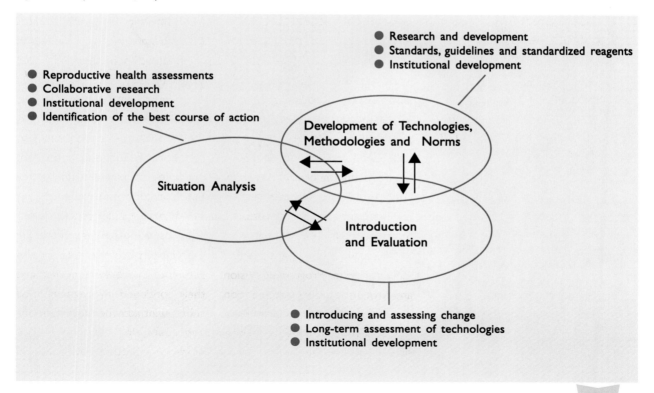

Mission Goals

The Programme's mission in improving reproductive health will be to:

- **Increase informed choices in reproductive health for women**
—by investigating and enhancing the understanding of women's reproductive health needs, particularly for fertility regulation and for quality of care;
—by developing and testing selected methods of fertility regulation in response to women's expressed needs at all stages of their reproductive life, including methods fully controlled and advocated by women;
—by pursuing research on contraceptive methods which prevent transmission of sexually transmitted diseases (including HIV), and thus may reduce infertility;
—by introducing methods in a manner which truly allows informed choice and improves quality of care;
—by establishing and monitoring that methods are appropriate, safe and used safely;
—by involving women in all aspects of the research process;
—by providing information that will increase women's awareness of sexual and reproductive health and encourage recognition of their sexual and reproductive rights;
—by investigating how gender roles attributed to women and men affect their sexual and reproductive health.

- **Increase male responsibility in reproductive health**
—by investigating and enhancing the understanding of the needs and attitudes of men and their roles in reproductive health, particularly in fertility regulation and in quality of care;
—by identifying new leads for methods of fertility regulation for men, including those that may prevent the transmission of sexually transmitted diseases (including HIV) and thus may reduce infertility;
—by developing, testing and introducing such methods and evaluating their long-term safety and acceptability;
—by providing information that will increase men's awareness of sexual and reproductive health and encourage their recognition of women's sexual and reproductive rights and thereby increase choices in better reproductive health for women;
—by investigating how gender roles attributed to women and men affect their sexual and reproductive health.

- **Respond to the needs of developing countries in research and capacity strengthening for research in reproductive health**
—to ensure that the needs of developing countries are reflected in all activities of the Programme;
—to support capacity building for research in reproductive health in order to:
  - facilitate the comprehensive assessment and continued monitoring of their reproductive health needs;
  - evaluate the needs of individuals and couples and the accessibility and performance of reproductive health care services, particularly in fertility regulation;
  - undertake the research required to address the needs identified and to participate in the global research effort;
  - promote ethical practices for research and for the introduction and use of reproductive health technologies.

- **Coordinate and expand the global research effort**
—by undertaking regular reviews of reproductive health research to identify critical needs and help establish research agendas;
—by stimulating innovative approaches to solving reproductive health problems;
—by collaborating with other agencies and within WHO in research in other areas of reproductive health, such as prevention of STDs and HIV, and safe motherhood;
—by mobilizing additional resources to the field;
—by contributing to a new partnership between the public and private sectors that will mobilize the resources and experience of industry in response to the identified research agendas while protecting the consumers.

health;
—reproductive behaviours;
—challenges inherent in the provision of services;
—assessment of contraceptive method mix and service infrastructure.

• *Institutional development*
—identification of the infrastructure required for a national research effort in the above areas.

• *Identifying the best course of action*
Information arising from the situation analysis can lead directly to changes in policy as well as the manner in which reproductive health services are provided. The analysis, however, can also point to the need for new and better technologies or methodologies and is thus essential to the setting of the Programme's research agenda in technology development.

Development of Technologies, Methodologies and Norms
The Programme pursues both biomedical and social science research on a variety of technologies relating to the control of fertility in women and in men and to the alleviation of reproductive health problems, such as infertility and reproductive tract infections including HIV/AIDS. This work also leads to the development of norms and standards. A unique feature of the Programme is the global network of collaborating centres that together undertake the large-scale clinical and epidemiological studies that are required for this work. The Programme collaborates with other international programmes in this field and has been able to draw upon

the experience and resources of the pharmaceutical industry while protecting the needs and interests of the public sector. Activities include:

• *Research and development*
—studies to understand the mechanisms underlying reproductive processes and to identify new leads;
—chemical synthesis, pharmacology and toxicology of new drugs;
—clinical trials and epidemiological studies;
—acceptability studies.

• *Standards, guidelines and standardized reagents*

—standardized laboratory procedures and reagents;
—drug regulatory requirements;
—ethical issues and standards.

• *Institutional development*
—maintenance and further development of the global network of collaborating centres.

Introduction and Evaluation
Research evaluates the impact of changes made to policy or to the delivery of reproductive health services as a result of the information gathered during the situation analysis or of the introduction of technologies. Activities in this area are at country level and are concerned also with longer-term assessments of safety and effectiveness and the strengthening of national research capacity.

• *Introducing and assessing change*
—reintroduction of under-utilized technologies;
—introduction of new technologies arising from the work of the

Programme or others;
—acceptability of methods being introduced;
—health services research and evaluation.

• *Long-term assessment of technologies*
—continuing assessment of contraceptive safety and effectiveness;
—post-marketing surveillance of new drugs and devices;
—interaction between fertility regulating methods and existing disease states including reproductive tract infections and HIV/AIDS.

• *Institutional development*
—support for the acquisition of research skills and facilities;
—participation in research activities outlined above.

Data from research activities in this third area can provide feedback to the other two areas that helps to shape the agenda for future work.

An interactive Programme

A conceptual model of the working structure of the Programme has been developed (see Fig. 2) which conveys a concept of integration and teamwork in the Programme's approach to its Mission Goals by linking the contributions of each Strategic Programme Component to each of the four goals. This structured approach will:

Fig. 2. Interactions between Programme components

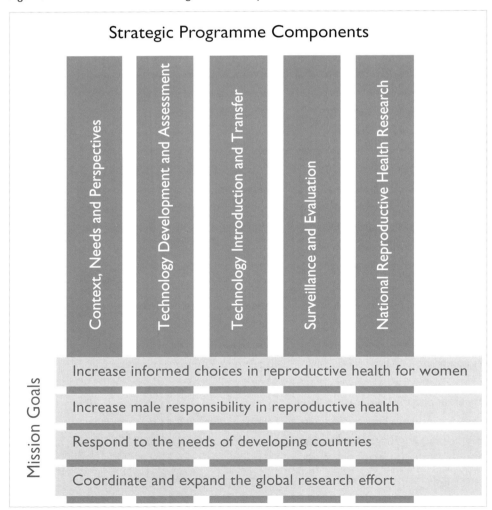

—reinforce horizontal links within the Programme;

—promote teamwork;

—facilitate a comprehensive response to reproductive health challenges together with other WHO programmes;

—provide the flexibility to respond to changes in demands and in finances; and

—allow the reporting of activities in terms of Mission Goals or of the individual Strategic Programme Components.

The interactive model has provided the basis for a revision of the Programme's organizational structure, governance and budgetary process, offering the Programme the flexibility to adapt effectively to meet the challenges of the future.

Mission Goals

The Mission Goals are the driving force for the Programme's work. They are a direct reflection of, and response to, the priorities being articulated by people, especially by women, through for example, the Programme of Action of the ICPD and the Platform for Action of the Fourth World Conference on Women (Beijing, September 1995). They set objectives, targets and milestones against which progress can be measured.

The Programme is establishing mechanisms for coordinating, promoting, monitoring and reporting on activities relating to each of the five Strategic Programme Components. The aim is to ensure these activities are linked effectively to meet the challenges inherent in the Mission Goals and the needs and perspectives of developing country people are reflected in the

outcomes of all Strategic Programme Components.

In contributing to the coordination and expansion of the global research effort, the Programme:

—promotes and coordinates its activities with other WHO programmes in implementing the Organization's comprehensive strategy in reproductive health;

—promotes close collaboration among key programmes in WHO by providing developing countries with the support they require to make a comprehensive assessment of needs for research and services in reproductive health;

—ensures linkage with cosponsors and all other agencies supporting research in relevant areas of reproductive health;

—contributes to the new partnership between the public and private sectors that seeks to draw industry back into contraceptive research and development;

—contributes to the development of standards, guidelines and norms in the area of reproductive health research, services and ethics.

Strategic Programme components

The technical work of the Programme will be undertaken within Strategic Programme Components that are sufficiently flexible to respond to changes in demands and finances. The Strategic Programme Components and their functions are as follows:

Context, needs and perspectives

• Conducts research aimed at determining expressed needs and perspectives concerning reproductive health issues and services, particularly in the area of fertility regulation.

- Identifies reproductive health problems and issues of a global nature and relevance and undertakes the necessary research to address them.

- Undertakes initiatives in areas of reproductive health identified by national or regional needs assessments, dependent upon the mobilization of additional financial resources.

Technology development and assessment

- Develops and tests selected methods of fertility regulation for women and for men.

- Identifies new leads for methods of fertility regulation.

- Conducts research on contraceptive methods which prevent transmission of sexually-transmitted diseases (including HIV), and which may reduce infertility.

- Develops biomedical and ethical standards and norms for the pre-clinical development and clinical testing of new technologies.

Introduction and transfer of technology

- Introduces new and under-utilized methods of fertility regulation, responding to users' needs and the capability of health care services.

- Coordinates activities with other agencies and mobilizes additional resources at country level.

- Works together with other Strategic Components of the Programme and with other WHO divisions in the comprehensive assessment of, and research on, re-productive health services within primary health care.

- Develops standards and norms on the quality of products for fertility regulation and for the introduction of methods into natio-nal programmes, taking into account ethical considerations.

Surveillance and evaluation

- Investigates issues of safety, efficacy and use of fertility regulating methods and the quality of care in their provision.

- Provides authoritative advice to policy-makers, providers and the public on issues of safety, efficacy and quality of care in fertility regulation.

- Undertakes surveillance and evaluation research initiatives in other areas of reproductive health which are related to the Programme's Mission Goals. (Research identified by national and regional needs assessments which is beyond the focus of the Programme would require the mobilization of additional funds.)

National reproductive health research

- Maintains and promotes the further development of the global network of centres with which the Programme collaborates to meet current standards of Good Clinical Practice.

- Collaborates with other Strategic Programme Components and with other WHO divisions in facilitating the comprehensive assessment of reproductive health needs.

- Promotes and strengthens the capacity for research on reproductive health problems identified for priority attention by countries and which fall within the strategic focus of the Programme.

- Mobilizes multilateral and

bilateral resources for country-level research and institutional development activities related to national research priorities, but which are outside the immediate focus of the Programme.

• Considers one or more regional initiatives to be planned and implemented in collaboration with other WHO programmes, the number and scope depending upon the funds available.

• Promotes the incorporation at national level of biomedical and ethical standards and norms developed by the Programme.

Technical support for research

The Programme's global research and institutional development activities depend for their success on the Clinical Trials and Informatics Support Group which:

—provides statistical and data processing support to the multinational clinical trials and epidemiological studies conducted by the Programme;

—provides informatics support to the administrative management of the Programme;

—strengthens the biostatistical and data processing capabilities of developing country institutions collaborating with the Programme to support their own reproductive health research; and

—contributes to the development of appropriate techniques for conducting multicentre research in reproductive health in developing countries.

Programme leadership and support

Three non-technical areas relate to all aspects of the Programme and are supportive of and contribute to the Programme's technical work.

Programme leadership

Programme leadership is responsible for the overall strategic direction of the Programme, for advocacy, fund-raising and public relations, for liaison with the governing body, and for coordination with other WHO divisions, the cosponsors and international programmes.

Information dissemination and communication

Information dissemination to the scientific community—already well taken care of by the many publications arising from the Programme—does not guarantee utilization of the research results. A greater effort is being made to ensure that information about the Programme reaches policy-makers and the public and is used effectively in the development and implementation of policy. Information about the work of the Programme and its positive impact on reproductive health will be central to the improved public relations strategy.

Support functions

This area of the Programme encompasses three activities:

• *Resource mobilization.* This is directed mainly at country-level activities including institutional strengthening and some activities under situation analysis, introduction and evaluation. The Programme seeks partnerships with other programmes and agencies and closer links with its cosponsors, offering the management of projects within the cosponsors' country and regional programmes.

- *Budgetary and financial management.*
- *Personnel management.*

The future—responding to change

In May 1995, the World Health Assembly endorsed the role of the Organization within the global reproductive health strategy and reaffirmed the unique role of the Organization with respect to advocacy, normative functions, research and technical cooperation in the area of reproductive health.

WHO's Executive Board, in January 1996, endorsed the Organization's plan to bring together, under the leadership of an Executive Director for Family and Reproductive Health, three large divisions, including the Programme, that deal with family and reproductive health. The Programme will be in close partnership with a new Division of Reproductive Health Technical Support and will have greater opportunity to increase its interaction with others in WHO having responsibility for programme development and technical support to countries. Three areas have been

identified for priority action in collaboration with the Technical Support Division. These are family planning, the reduction of maternal mortality and morbidity and reproductive tract infections including STDS. Other areas under consideration include violence against women, female genital mutilation and research relevant to currently underserved groups such as adolescents and people in refugee situations. The Programme's closer interaction with country-level activities is likely to result in greater attention to operations research, information from which will enhance the quality of the support that the Organization will be able to provide to its Member States.

The broad mandate approved in June 1995 allows for such developments. Equally important, the new conceptual framework for the Programme, in which its four Mission Goals are interlinked with five Strategic Programme Components, has an inherent adaptability which allows easy expansion in response to future research challenges.

Funding during 1994–1995

In June 1993 the Programme's Policy and Coordination Committee approved a budget of some US$ 51.9 million for the biennium 1994–1995. However, as it became clear that contributions to the Programme would not reach that level, a revised budget was prepared at US$ 41.2 million. The actual contributions during the biennium reached US$ 41.2 million. This represented a decrease of about US$ 5.3 million compared to the amount available in 1992–1993.

Fig. 1 compares the actual contributions received by the Programme in relation to approved budgets since 1986. The contributions received are also represented as a percentage of the approved budget for each biennium. In terms of trend, the actual contributions for each biennium were close to 90% of the approved budgets during the period 1986-1991. During the last two biennia, the percentage reached 78% and 79% only.

Contributions

The sources of contributions received by the Programme during the last biennium and the total since 1970 are shown in Table 1. In 1994–1995, 24 governments and agencies (including WHO

through its regular budget) contributed US$ 41 161 400 (US$ 19 984 000 in 1994 and US$ 21 177 400 in 1995). The donors included 13 developed countries, five developing countries and six agencies/organizations. New Zealand contributed for the first time.

As can be seen from Table 1, the Programme remains heavily dependent on a relatively small number of "core contributors". In 1994-1995 the three largest donors were the United Kingdom, UNFPA, and the USA, providing some 56% of the total contributions.

The contributions made by the developing countries, though small, are an important sign of those countries' continued interest in the work of the Programme. In fact, the developing countries contribute more than the amounts shown in the Table. For instance, in order to maintain certain research institutions the developing countries make "counterpart contributions". Since funds made available to the institutions by the Programme often do not cover all the costs, the institutions frequently pay for some of the staff time spent on, and materials used in, Programme projects. These contributions are difficult to quantify, but are certainly substantial in many cases.

Table 1. Income for 1994 and 1995 and for the period 1970-1995 (in US$ thousands)

Source of funds	1994	1995	1970–1995
I. Developed countries			
Australia	505.8	537.7	3 544.0
Canada	292.0	283.7	9 280.6
Denmark	1 941.0	-	29 514.5
Finland	-	117.3	2 825.8
France	-	-	6.5
Germany	365.0	466.4	13 143.8
Italy	127.4	167.7	554.9
Netherlands	422.8	622.8	5 097.7
New Zealand	-	13.2	13.2
Norway	1 147.2	1 231.1	43 390.5
Russian Federation (in kind)	-	-	99.5
Sweden	1 312.3	688.7	92 079.0
Switzerland	279.7	391.3	2 728.1
United Kingdom	3 961.9	3 919.4	60 692.1
United States of America	2 750.0	2 750.0	11 220.6
II. Developing countries			
Argentina	-	-	45.1
Bangladesh	-	-	5.0
Chile	-	-	35.0
China	55.0	55.0	710.0
Cuba	-	-	24.6
India	-	35.4	626.1
Kenya	-	-	0.5
Malaysia	-	-	1.1
Mexico	3.9	3.9	90.6
Nigeria	5.3	-	60.8
Pakistan	-	-	5.0
Thailand	7.5	20.0	121.6
III. Cosponsors, foundations, etc.			
Family Health International	-	-	205.0
Ford Foundation	30.0	9.0	1084.0
IDRC (Canada)	-	-	716.5
Rockefeller Foundation	675.0	30.0	3 247.9
UNDP	282.5	282.5	1 695.0
UNFPA	3 500.0	3 500.0	48 040.0
UNFPA funds for country and inter-country projects	1 341.6	1 187.2	22 588.5
World Bank	-	3 750.0	19 258.3
IV. WHO and miscellaneous			
WHO	769.8	769.8	12 817.4
Interest	127.8	302.4	11 074.7
Handling charge for reagents and miscellaneous	80.5	42.9	1 280.2
Patents	-	-	68.9
Total income	**19 984.0**	**21 177.4**	**397 992.6**

Fig. I. Funds received in relation to approved budgets during 1986–1995

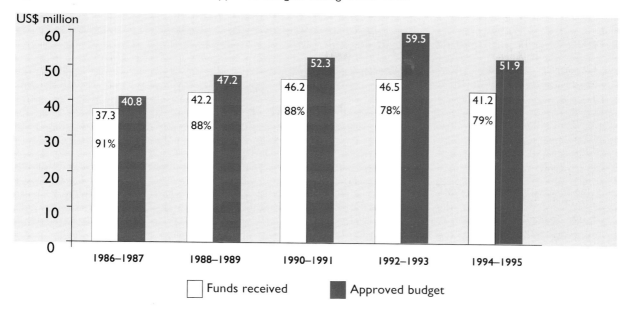

Annex 2

Centres collaborating with HRP during 1994–1995

WHO African Region

Benin
    National University of Benin, Cotonou

Botswana
    National Institute of Development and Research Documentation, Gaborone

Burundi
    University Research Centre for Economic and Social Development (CURDES), Bujumbura

Cameroon
    Hospital and University Centre of Yaoundé, Yaoundé
    Institute for Training and Research in Demography (IFORD), Yaoundé

Ethiopia
    Addis Ababa University, Addis Ababa

Ghana
    Institute of African Studies, Legon
    University of Ghana Medical School, Accra

Kenya
    Institute of Primate Research, Karen, Nairobi
    Kenya Medical Research Institute, Nairobi
    Kenyatta National Hospital, Nairobi
    Moi University, Eldoret
    National Museums of Kenya, Nairobi
    University of Nairobi, Nairobi

Mali
    Population and Development Research Centre, Bamako

Mauritius
    Mauritius Family Planning Association, Port Louis

Mozambique
    Maputo Central Hospital, School of Medicine, Maputo

Nigeria
    Ahmadu Bello University, Zaria
    Lagos State University, Lagos
    National Planning Commission, Lagos
    National Population Commission, Lagos
    Obafemi Awolowo University, Ile-Ife
    Ogun State University, Sagamu
    University of Benin, Teaching Hospital, Benin City
    University of Ibadan, Ibadan

Rwanda
    Regional Centre for Training and Research in Family Health, Kigali

Senegal
Ministry of Public Health and Social Welfare, Dakar
University of Dakar, Faculty of Medicine and Pharmacy, Dakar

Sierra Leone
Connaught Hospital, Freetown
Princess Christian Maternity Hospital, Freetown

Togo
University of Benin, Lomé

Uganda
Makerere University Medical School, Kampala

United Republic of Tanzania
Family Planning Association of Tanzania (UMATI), Dar-es-Salaam
Muhimbili Medical Centre, Faculty of Medicine, Dar-es-Salaam

Zaire
Technical Information and Research Centre for Development, Kinshasa
University of Kinshasa, Faculty of Demography, Kinshasa

Zambia
Family Life Movement of Zambia, Lusaka
Planned Parenthood Association of Zambia, Lusaka
University Teaching Hospital, Lusaka
University of Zambia, School of Medicine, Lusaka

Zimbabwe
University of Zimbabwe, Harare

WHO Region of the Americas

Argentina
Centre for Endocrinological Investigations (CEDIE), Buenos Aires

Centre for Population Studies (CENEP), Buenos Aires
Centre for Reproductive Biology (CBR), Rosario
Centre for Research and Promotion of Health and Environment (CIPSA), Buenos Aires
Centre for Studies in Endocrinology (CEEN), La Plata
Centre for Studies of the State and Society (CEDES), Buenos Aires
Foundation for Contemporary Studies (FUNDECO), Buenos Aires
Institute of Biology and Experimental Medicine, Buenos Aires
Norberto Quirno Centre for Medical Education and Clinical Investigations (CEMIC), Buenos Aires
Reproduction and Lactation Laboratory (LARLAC), Mendoza
Rosario Centre of Perinatal Studies (CREP), Rosario
SAMIC Paediatric Hospital, Buenos Aires
University of Buenos Aires, Buenos Aires

Bolivia
Institute of Human Genetics, Major University of San Andres, La Paz

Brazil
Campinas Research Centre for the Control of Maternal and Childhood Diseases (CEMICAMP), Campinas
Centre for Population Studies, Campinas
Federal University of Bahia, Maternity Climerio de Oliveira, Salvador
Federal University of Juiz de Fora, Centre for Reproductive Biology, Juiz de Fora

Federal University of Pernambuco, Centre for Biological Sciences, Recife
Federal University of Rio Grande do Sol, Porto Alegre
Institute of Health of Sao Paulo, State Secretariat of Health, Sao Paulo
National School of Public Health, Oswaldo Cruz Foundation, Rio de Janeiro
Paulista School of Medicine, Sao Paulo
School of Medicine of Sao Paulo, Sao Paulo
State Secretariat of Health, Sao Paulo
State University of Rio de Janeiro, Rio de Janeiro

Canada

Institute Armand-Frappier, Laval-des-Rapides, Quebec
McGill University, Montreal
McMaster University, Hamilton
University of Montreal, Maissonneuve-Rosemont Hospital, Montreal

Chile

Catholic University of Chile, Santiago
Chilean Association for Family Welfare (APROFA), Santiago
Chilean Institute of Reproductive Medicine (ICMER), Santiago
Chilean Society of Sexual Research and Sex Education, Santiago
Education for Improvement of Quality of Life (EDUK), Santiago
Frontier University, Medical Faculty, Temuco
Institute for Mother and Child (IDIMI), University of Chile, Santiago
Jose Joaquin Aguirre Hospital, Santiago
Latin American Institute of Health and Population, Santiago
Los Alimentos Institute of Nutrition and Technology, Santiago
Paula Jaraquemada Hospital, University of Chile, Santiago
Programme for Support and Outreach in Maternal and Child Health, Santiago
Ramon Barros Luco-Trudeau Hospital, Santiago
San Borja Arriaran Clinical Hospital, Santiago
Southern Division of Medical Sciences, Santiago
Southern University of Chile, Valdivia
Support Programme for the Extension of Health, Santiago
University of Chile, Clinical Hospital, Santiago
University of Chile, Faculty of Medicine, Santiago
University of Valparaiso, Medical School, Valparaiso

Colombia

External University of Colombia, Bogota
Profamilia, Bogota
University Hospital of Valle, Cali
Unit for Maternal Health Orientation and Assistance (ORIENTAME), Bogota
University of Valle, Cali

Costa Rica

Demographic Association of Costa Rica (CENDEISS), San José

Cuba

Cmdte. Fajardo Hospital, Havana
National Centre for Sex Education, Havana
Pedro Kouri Institute of Tropical Medicine, Havana
Ramon Gonzalez Coro Hospital, Havana

Dominican Republic

Dominican Association for Family Welfare (Profamilia), Santo Domingo

Guatemala

Centre for Epidemiological Research, Guatemala City
El Valle University of Guatemala, Guatemala City

Institute of Nutrition of Central America and Panama (INCAP), Guatemala City

Jamaica
Ministry of Health, Kingston

Mexico
Centre for Research and Advanced Studies of the IPN, Mexico City
Centre for Studies in Population and Informatics (CEPM), Mexico City
General Directorate of Family Planning, Secretariat of Health, Mexico City
Mexican Academy for Research and Medical Demography, Mexico City
Mexican Association of Sex Education, Mexico City
Mexican Institute for Family and Population Research, Mexico City
Mexican Institute of Social Security, Mexico City
Mexican Institute of Social Studies, Mexico City
Mexican Interuniversity Group for Epidemiological Research in Reproductive Health (GIMIESAR), Durango
Mexican School of Public Health, Mexico City
National Institute of Public Health, Cuernavaca
Regional Centre for Multidisciplinary Investigations (CRIM), Morelos
Salvador Zubiran National Institute of Nutrition, Mexico City
University of Guanajuato, Mexico City
University Hospital, University of Coahuila at Torreon, Torreon

Panama
Center for Research in Human Reproduction (CRHR), Ministry of Health, Panama

Paraguay
Centre for Rural Studies of Itapua, Asunciøn

Peru
Association of Professionals for the Promotion of Maternal and Child Health, Lima
Cayetano Heredia National University Hospital, Lima
Pedro Ruiz Gallo National University, Chiclayo

United States of America
College of Physicians and Surgeons, New York, NY
Cornell University, Ithaca, NY
Harbor-UCLA Medical Center, UCLA School of Medicine, Torrance, CA
Harvard Medical School, Boston, MA
Johns Hopkins University, Baltimore, MD
M.D. Anderson Cancer Center, Houston, TX
Massachusetts General Hospital, Boston, MA
Mayo Foundation, Mayo Medical School, Rochester, MN
Medical College of Georgia, Augusta, GA
Medisorb Technologies International, Cincinnati, OH
Ohio State University Research Foundation, Columbus, OH
Peninsula Laboratories, Inc., Belmont, NC
Pennsylvania State University, The Milton S. Hershey Medical Center, Hershey, PA
Population Council, New York, NY
Program for Appropriate Technology for Health, Seattle, WA
Research Foundation of State University of New York, New York, NY
Research Triangle Institute, Chemistry and Life Sciences Group, Research Triangle Park, NC
San Francisco General Hospital, San Francisco, CA
Southern Research Institute, Birmingham, AL
The Regents of University of California, Irvine, CA
Thomas Jefferson University, Philadelphia, PN
Tufts University, Medford, MA
University of Austin, Austin, TX
University of California, Davis California Primate Research Center, Davis, CA
University of Iowa, Iowa City, IO

University of Michigan, Ann Arbor, MI
University of Minnesota, Minneapolis, MN
University of North Carolina, Chapel Hill, NC
University of South Florida, Tampa, FL
University of Washington, Seattle, WA

Uruguay
Centre for Information and Research of Uruguay (CIESU), Montevideo

Venezuela
Concepcion Palacios Maternity, Caracas
Foundation for Mother and Infant Studies (FUNDAMATIN), Caracas
Simon Bolivar University, Caracas

WHO Eastern Mediterranean Region

Egypt
Assiut University, Faculty of Medicine, Assiut
Egyptian Fertility Care Society, Cairo
International Islamic Center for Population Studies and Research, Cairo
Shatby Maternity Hospital, Alexandria
University of Alexandria, Alexandria

Pakistan
National Research Institute of Fertility Control (NRIFC), Karachi

Sudan
University of Khartoum, Faculty of Medicine, Khartoum

Tunisia
National Office for Family and Population, Tunis
Research Centre for Human Reproduction, Tunis

WHO European Region

Armenia
Armenian Research Centre for Maternal and Child Health Protection, Yerevan

Belgium
Clinical Chemistry Laboratory, Brugge
Institute of Demography, Catholic University, Louvain-la-Neuve

Denmark
Danish Cancer Registry, Danish Cancer Society, Copenhagen
University of Copenhagen, Copenhagen

Finland
Finnish Student Health Service, Helsinki
University of Kuopio, Kuopio
University of Turku, Turku

France
Hormonal Molecular Pathology (INSERM), Lyon
Institute of Political Studies, Paris
Medical Information Centre of the Civil Hospices of Lyon, Lyon
National Institute of Health and Medical Research, Nice
University of South Paris, Le Kremlin-Bicêtre, Paris

Georgia

Institute of Experimental Pathology and Therapy, Sukhumi
Zhordania Institute of Human Reproduction, Tbilisi

Germany

Centre for Epidemiology and Health Research, Berlin
Ernst-Moritz-Arndt University, Greifswald
Institute of Hormone and Fertility Research, Hamburg
Max Planck Clinical Research Institute of Reproductive Medicine, Münster
Medical Facilities of the University of Düsseldorf, Düsseldorf
University of Münster, Women's Clinic, Münster

Hungary

Albert Szent-Gyorgyi Medical University, Szeged
Institute of Microbiology, University Medical School, Pecs

Israel

Beilinson Medical Center Sackler School of Medicine, Petah-Tiqva
Chaim Sheba Medical Centre, Tel Aviv
Soroka University Hospital, Beer Sheva

Italy

Ambrosian Centre for Natural Methods (CAMEN), Milan
University of Milan, Faculty of Medicine, Milan
University of Turin, Turin

Netherlands

Alphatron Medical Systems B.V., Rotterdam
Central Laboratory for Clinical Chemistry, Groningen
Central Veterinary Institute, Lelystad
Erasmus University, Rotterdam
Netherlands Cancer Institute, Amsterdam

Poland

Polish Academy of Sciences, Poznan

Russian Federation

Institute of Experimental Endocrinology and Hormone Chemistry, Moscow
Research Centre for Obstetrics, Gynaecology and Perinatology, Moscow
Russian Academy of Medical Sciences, St Petersburg

Slovenia

University Institute of Public Health, Ljubljana
University of Ljubljana Medical Centre, Ljubljana

Sweden

Galenus AB, Uppsala
International Child Health Unit, Uppsala
Karolinska Institute, Stockholm
Uppsala University, Uppsala

Switzerland

Cantonal Hospital, University of Geneva, Geneva

Turkey

Hacettepe University, School of Medicine, Ankara
University of Istanbul, School of Medicine, Istanbul

ANNEX 2

Ukraine
Kiev Research Institute of Endocrinology and Metabolism, Kiev

United Kingdom of Great Britain and Northern Ireland
Birmingham Maternity Hospital, Queen Elizabeth II Medical Centre, Birmingham
Cambridge University, Cambridge
City of London Polytechnic, London
City University, London
Department of Pharmacology, University of Edinburgh, Edinburgh
Hammersmith Hospital, London
Hazleton Laboratories UK, Harrogate
Huntingdon Research Centre, Huntingdon
Institute of Cancer Research, London
Institute of Zoology, the Zoological Society of London, London
Inveresk Research International Ltd., Musselburgh
Kerfoot Pharmaceuticals, Ashton-under-Lyne
King's College Hospital Medical School, London
Lothian Health Board, Family Planning and Well Woman Services, Edinburgh
Ludwig Institute of Cancer Research, St Mary's Hospital Medical School, London
Micron Mills Ltd., Orpington
Oxford University, Oxford
Palatine Centre, Manchester
Palmer Research Ltd., Honeywell
Radcliffe Infirmary, Oxford
Reference Laboratory for Anticoagulant Reagents and Control, Manchester
Roussel Laboratories Ltd., Uxbridge
Southampton General Hospital, University of Southampton, Southampton
The Princess Royal Hospital, Royal Hull Hospitals, Hull
University of Aberdeen, Aberdeen
University of Bristol, School of Medical Sciences, Bristol
University College and Middlesex School of Medicine, London
University of Edinburgh, Centre for Reproductive Biology, Edinburgh
University of Exeter, Institute of Population Studies, Exeter
University of Glasgow, Glasgow
University of Liverpool Medical School, Liverpool
University of London, London
University of Manchester, Manchester
Warwick University, Department of Chemistry, Coventry

Uzbekistan
Uzbekistan Research Institute of Obstetrics and Gynaecology, Tashkent

Yugoslavia
University of Belgrade, Clinical Center of the School of Medicine, Belgrade

WHO South-East Asia Region

Bangladesh
Bangladesh Association for Prevention of Septic Abortion (BAPSA), Dhaka
Bangladesh Institute of Research for Promotion of Essential and Reproductive Health Technologies
(BIRPERHT), Dhaka
Development Assistance Council, Dhaka
International Centre for Diarrhoeal Disease Research, Bangladesh (ICDDR,B), Dhaka

Democratic People's Republic of Korea
Pyongyang Maternity Hospital, Pyongyang

India

    All India Institute of Medical Sciences, New Delhi
    Centre for Operations Research and Training (CORT), Baroda
    Indian Council of Medical Research, New Delhi
    Indian Institute of Management, Bangalore
    Indian Institute of Science, Bangalore
    Institute for Research in Reproduction, Bombay
    K.E.M. Hospital Research Centre, Pune
    National Institute of Health and Family Welfare, New Delhi
    Nuclear Medicine and Radioimmunoassay Unit, Agra
    Population Research Centre, Faculty of Science, Baroda
    Postgraduate Institute of Basic Medical Sciences, Madras
    University of Baroda, Baroda
    University College of Medical Sciences and G.T.B Hospital, New Delhi

Indonesia

    Airlangga University, Dr Soetomo Hospital, Surabaya
    Center for Social and Cultural Studies, Institute of Sciences (PMB-LIPI), Jakarta
    Faculty of Economics, Demographic Institute, Jakarta
    Gadjah Mada University, Faculty of Medicine, Yogyakarta
    National Family Planning Coordinating Board (BKKBN), Jakarta
    Padjadjaran University, Human Reproduction Study Group, Bandung
    Sriwijaya University, Faculty of Medicine, Palembang
    University of Indonesia, Jakarta
    Yayasan Kusuma Buana, Jakarta

Maldives

    Ministry of Health and Welfare, Male

Mongolia

    State Research Centre on MCH and Human Reproduction, Ulaanbaatar

Myanmar

    Ministry of Health, Department of Medical Research, Yangon

Nepal

    Integrated Development Systems, Kathmandu
    Tribhuvan University, Institute of Medicine, Kathmandu

Sri Lanka

    Family Planning Association of Sri Lanka, Colombo
    University of Colombo, Colombo
    University of Ruhuna, Matara

Thailand

    Chiang Mai University Research Institute for Health, Chiang Mai
    Chulalongkorn Hospital Medical School, Bangkok
    Institute of Health Research, Bangkok
    Institute of Population and Social Research, Nakhon Pathom
    Khon Kaen University, Faculty of Medicine, Khon Kaen
    Mahidol University, Bangkok
    Ministry of Public Health, National Family Planning Programme, Bangkok
    Mother and Child Hospital, Health Promotion Center, Khon Kaen
    Prince of Songkla University, Faculty of Medicine, Hat Yai
    Ramathibodi Hospital, Bangkok
    Siriraj Family Planning Research Center, Bangkok
    Siriraj Hospital, Bangkok
    Thai Red Cross Society, Centre for AIDS Research, Bangkok
    The Concept Foundation, Bangkok

ANNEX 2

WHO Western Pacific Region

Australia
Flinders University of South Australia, Bedford Park
Monash University, Clayton, Melbourne
Prince Henry's Institute of Medical Research, Melbourne
Royal Prince Alfred Hospital, Sydney
St. Michael Research Foundation, Melbourne
Sydney Centre for Reproductive Health Research, Ashfield
University of Newcastle, Newcastle
University of Sydney, Sydney
Westmead Hospital, Westmead

China
Beijing Medical University, Beijing
East China Normal University, Population Research Institute, Shanghai
Family Planning Research Institute of Guangdong, Guangzhou
Family Planning Research Institute of Sichuan, Chengdu
Family Planning Research Institute, Tong Ji Medical University, Wuhan
Family Planning Research Institute of Zhejiang, Hangzhou
First Teaching Hospital, Beijing Medical University, Beijing
Harbin University of Medical Sciences, Harbin
Institute of Population Research, Peking University, Beijing
Institute of Zoology, Academy of Sciences, Beijing
International Peace MCH Hospital, Shanghai
Jiangsu Family Planning Research Institute, Nanjing
Kunming Institute of Zoology, Academy of Sciences, Kunming
National Evaluation Centre for the Toxicology of Fertility Regulating Drugs, Shanghai
National Research Institute for Family Planning, Beijing
Obstetrics and Gynaecology Hospital, Beijing
Peking Union Medical College Hospital, Beijing
Ren Ji Hospital, Shanghai
Shanghai Institute of Cell Biology, Shanghai
Shanghai Institute of Materia Medica, Shanghai
Shanghai Institute of Planned Parenthood Research, Shanghai
Shanghai Medical University, Shanghai
Shanghai Second Medical University, Shanghai
Shanxi Provincial People's Hospital, Shanxi
Tianjin Medical College, Tianjin
Tianjin Municipal Research Institute for Family Planning, Tianjin
Xin Hua Hospital, Shanghai Second Medical College, Shanghai
Xuan-Wu Hospital, Capital Institute of Medicine, Beijing
Zhong Shan Hospital, Shanghai Medical University, Shanghai

Hong Kong
Chinese University of Hong Kong, Faculty of Medicine, Hong Kong
University of Hong Kong, Queen Mary Hospital, Hong Kong

Japan
Keio University School of Medicine, Tokyo

Malaysia
University of Malaysia, Faculty of Economics and Administration, Kuala Lumpur

New Zealand
Massey University, Palmerston North

Papua New Guinea
Papua New Guinea Institute of Medical Research, Goroka

Philippines

Dr. Jos, Fabella Memorial Hospital, Manila
Management Communications System, Quezon City
Notre Dame University, Cotabato City
Reproductive Health Care Centre, Manila
Silliman University, Dumaguete City
University of the Philippines, College of Medicine, Manila

Republic of Korea

Chonnam National University, Kwangju
Institute of Health and Environment Science, Seoul National University, Seoul
Institute of Population and Health Services Research, Yonsei University, Seoul
Institute of Reproductive Medicine and Population, Seoul National University, Seoul
Korea Institute for Health and Social Affairs, Seoul
Population and Development Studies Centre, Seoul National University, Seoul

Singapore

National University of Singapore, Singapore
Singapore General Hospital, Singapore

Viet Nam

Hung Vuong Hospital, Ho Chi Minh City
Institute for the Protection of Mother and Child, Hanoi
Institute of Sociology, Hanoi
National Committee for Population and Family Planning (NCPFP), Hanoi

HRP staff (December 1995)

Director's Office
Dr Giuseppe Benagiano, Director
Dr Paul Van Look, Associate Director
Mrs Stephanie Baron, Administrative Officer
Miss Corinne Anderson, Secretary
Mrs Lee Yoke-Wan, Secretary

Resource Mobilization
Dr Francis Webb, Scientist
Ms Jennifer Bayley, Secretary

Laboratory Methods Group
Dr Paul Van Look, Acting Manager
Miss Sybil Taylor, Secretary

Toxicology Panel
Dr Patrick Rowe, Acting Manager
Miss Sybil Taylor, Secretary

Scientific and Ethical Review Group
Mr David Griffin, Acting Manager
Mrs Lynda Pasini, Secretary

Communication and Dissemination of Information
Mr Jitendra Khanna, Technical Officer
Mrs Christel Karner-Wortmann, Clerk

Women's perspectives
Ms Jane Cottingham, Technical Officer
Mrs Pamela Jamieson, Secretary*

Unit of Administration and Finance
Mr Einar Röed, Chief
Mrs Diana Fortune, Administrative Assistant
Mrs Annie Le Guenne, Administrative Assistant
Mr Luc Bernier, Photocopying Clerk
Miss Natalie Netty-Marbell, Secretary*

*Temporary staff.

Equipment and Supplies

    Mrs Teresa Harmand, Clerk

Research and Development

    Dr Paul Van Look, Responsible Officer

    Mrs Hazel Ziaei, Administrative Assistant

    Miss Sybil Taylor, Secretary

Unit of Technology Development and Assessment

    Dr Paul Van Look, Acting Chief

    Mrs Hazel Ziaei, Administrative Assistant

Task Force on Long-acting Systemic Agents for Fertility Regulation

    Dr Catherine d'Arcangues, Task Force Manager

    Mrs Karie Pellicer, Secretary

Task Force on Post-ovulatory Methods of Fertility Regulation

    Dr Paul Van Look, Task Force Manager

    Dr Helena von Hertzen, Assistant Task Force Manager

    Mrs Janette Marozzi, Secretary

Task Force on Methods for the Regulation of Male Fertility

    Mr David Griffin, Acting Task Force Manager

    Mrs Lynn Sellaro, Secretary

Task Force on Vaccines for Fertility Regulation

    Mr David Griffin, Task Force Manager

    Mrs Lynda Pasini, Secretary

Task Force on Methods for the Natural Regulation of Fertility

    Dr Paul Van Look, Acting Task Force Manager

    Dr Helena von Hertzen, Acting Assistant Task Force Manager

    Dr Catherine d'Arcangues, Acting Assistant Task Force Manager

    Mrs Jenny Perrin, Secretary (half-time)

Task Force on the Prevention and Management of Infertility

    Dr Patrick Rowe, Task Force Manager

    Ms Barbara Kayser, Secretary

Research Group on Intrauterine Devices

    Dr Patrick Rowe, Manager

    Mrs Jenny Perrin, Secretary (half-time)

ANNEX 3

Unit of Technology Introduction and Transfer
(Task Force on Research on Introduction and Transfer of Technologies for Fertility Regulation)

Mr Peter Hall, Chief/Task Force Manager
Dr Peter Fajans, Scientist
Mrs Ruth Malaguti, Secretary (half-time)
Ms Nicola Sabatini, Secretary

Unit of Epidemiological Research
(Task Force for Epidemiological Research on Reproductive Health)

Dr Olav Meirik, Chief
Mrs Anne Allemand, Secretary

Unit of Social Science Research
(Task Force for Social Science Research on Reproductive Health)

Dr Iqbal Shah, Acting Chief
Dr Cynthia Indriso, Consultant*
Ms Maud Keizer, Secretary

Unit of Statistics and Data Processing

Dr Olusola Ayeni, Chief
Dr Timothy Farley, Statistician
Dr Gilda Piaggio Pareja, Statistician

Mr Alain Pinol, Senior System Analyst
Mr Alexandre Peregoudov, Analyst Programmer
Mr Isaac Olayinka, Analyst Programmer *

Miss Simone Boccard, Statistical Assistant
Mrs Annie Chevrot, Statistical Assistant (half-time)
Miss Catherine Hazelden, Statistical Assistant
Miss Nicole Laperrière, Statistical Assistant
Mr Frederick Schlagenhaft, Statistical Assistant
Mrs Vivienne Strahle, Data Processing Assistant
Ms Milena Vucurevic, Statistical Assistant

Mrs Evelyn Jiguet, Secretary
Mrs Gabrielle Puget, Data-entry Operator
Mrs Yvonne-Marie Towobola, Data-entry Operator

Information Systems/Microcomputers
Mr Ed Hulseman, Clerk

*Temporary staff.

Resources for Research
(Unit of Essential National Research)

       Dr Joseph Kasonde, Responsible Officer

       Mrs Hazel Ziaei, Administrative Assistant

Africa and Eastern Mediterranean

       Dr Wole Akande, Programme Manager

       Dr Heli Bathija, Scientist

       Ms Margrit Kaufmann, Secretary

       Mrs Catherine Blanc, Secretary (half-time)*

Latin America and the Caribbean

       Dr José Villar, Programme Manager

       Dr Enrique Ezcurra, Consultant*

       Mrs Joyce Starks, Secretary

       Ms Brenda Curina, Secretary

Asia and Pacific

       Dr Chander Puri, Consultant*

       Dr Yi Fei Wang, Consultant*

       Mrs Barbara Fontaine, Secretary

       Miss Sybil Taylor, Secretary

Eastern Europe

       Dr Joseph Kasonde, Acting Programme Manager

       Mrs Hazel Zaiei, Administrative Assistant

*Temporary staff.